Don't Let Anyone Take Your Joy Away

Don't Let Anyone Take Your Joy Away

An inside look at Negro League baseball and its legacy

Stanley Glenn

Stanley Glenn

President, Negro League Baseball Players Association

iUniverse, Inc.

New York Lincoln Shanghai

Don't Let Anyone Take Your Joy Away
An inside look at Negro League baseball and its legacy

iUniverse books may be ordered through booksellers or by contacting:

iUniverse
2021 Pine Lake Road, Suite 100
Lincoln, NE 68512
www.iuniverse.com
1-800-Authors (1-800-288-4677)

ISBN-13: 978-0-595-40075-1 (pbk)
ISBN-13: 978-0-595-67777-1 (cloth)
ISBN-13: 978-0-595-84459-3 (ebk)
ISBN-10: 0-595-40075-2 (pbk)
ISBN-10: 0-595-67777-0 (cloth)
ISBN-10: 0-595-84459-6 (ebk)

Printed in the United States of America

This book is dedicated to my beloved family:

My wife, Vera,

Our son, Stanley, Jr., and

my daughter, Lisa.

Table of Contents

Acknowledgments

Without inspiration and input from certain individuals, this book might never have been written and published. So I want to offer special thanks to the late Emmanuel "Menschy" Goldblatt, my coach at John Bartram High School, who gave me my start in baseball, and was like a second father to me.

Thanks also to the entire Philadelphia Stars team, especially my buddies Mahlon Duckett, Hal Gould, and Bill Cash, and those no longer with us. I couldn't have asked for better teammates, on the field and in life.

I am also grateful to the Business Association of West Parkside, Philadelphia, especially president Marjorie Ogilvie and treasurer Miller Parker, whose sponsorship helped replace a piece of American history that's been missing from the bookshelves.

And finally, special thanks to my manuscript editor, Miranda Spencer, for helping me flesh out and structure my story into the book you now hold in your hands.

Foreword

Stanley Glenn's book, *"Don't Let Anyone Take Your Joy Away: An inside look at Negro League Baseball and its legacy,"* gives an intimate and in-depth look at the experience of Negro League Baseball players. I believe most people like me who were born after the Civil Rights Movement cannot comprehend the struggles that African Americans endured to attain equality under the law. In this day and age, we can't imagine baseball without Barry Bonds, Darryl Strawberry, or Ken Griffey, Jr., and we take for granted that Black athletes have the same opportunities to excel as their White counterparts. This book caused me to realize and appreciate the proud legacy of Negro League Baseball.

Mr. Glenn tells the story from his perspective, and invites the reader into his personal journey, through the daily trials and tribulations of a Negro League Baseball player. His detailed anecdotes about the indignities he and his teammates suffered at the hands of Jim Crow struck a nerve in me. To spend a night in jail, or to be denied gas and oil for your vehicle and air for your tires for no reason other than the color of your skin, is something that I cannot fathom and that I am fortunate to never have endured. For myself, someone who has never experienced overt, institutionalized racism, Mr. Glenn's story brings the cruelty of the Jim Crow era to reality.

Although I was heartbroken by the brutal injustice that these heroes faced, I was inspired by their strength and determination to continue in spite of the forces against them. They persevered for the love of the game. Mr. Glenn thoroughly expresses their devotion to the game of baseball, so much so that reading this book made me want to pick up a ball and glove. Despite the constant adversities these men faced, they enjoyed their historic journey, and came away with treasured memories and lifelong friendships. Through his blend of humorous anecdotes, inspiring words of wisdom, and colorful imagery, Mr. Glenn wonderfully conveys the bittersweet paradox that was the Negro League Baseball experience.

Until I read this book, I was unaware of how important the Negro Leagues were to the Black community and to the world of baseball. They instilled pride and hope in African Americans in the early 20th century, and continue to be an inspiration to many like myself today. The recruitment of great players from the Negro Leagues into the Major Leagues, beginning with Jackie Robinson in 1947, almost single-handedly saved several teams from bankruptcy, and has allowed Major League Baseball to continue today. Mr. Glenn's book is a moving, compelling story that I would recommend to young people, historians, sports fans of all ages, and anyone touched by the strength and will of the human spirit. This book has given me a newfound respect for the unsung heroes of Negro League Baseball.

Aaliyah Green
Rutgers University student

Introduction

Why I Wrote This Book

One evening several years ago, I traveled to visit Josh, one of the grandsons of a coworker at my last employer, Penn Electrical Supply. The little fellow was all of five years old, but already he was a big Philadelphia sports fan. He knew all the players on the Phillies and the Eagles teams, and felt quite at home with me because he had begun collecting memorabilia from my former team, the Philadelphia Stars, who played during the heyday of Negro League Baseball.

Quite naturally, Josh had asked his father, *why* there was a Negro League and a Big League in America. This precious little boy knew nothing about segregation or racism. White, black, or brown, baseball players were all just heroes to him. My friend said he did not know what to tell his son, and asked if I would help explain. So I did.

There are many Joshes in this world, not all of them children. As I round the corner on 80 years old, I often speak about the Stars and Negro League Baseball at schools, churches, and community centers in the Delaware Valley and up and down the Eastern Seaboard. My audience is kids and adults who are unaware of this important piece of American history. Patiently, plainly, and with great pride, I tell our story.

Baseball lovers around the world have heard of Jackie Robinson, yet right here in the United States of America, I have met black ballplayers in the Major League who know little or nothing about this pioneer. This saddens me: How can they know who they are if they don't know where they came from?

It's clear to me that we—black families and white—have not taught our children about the Negro Major Leagues. It's rarely taught in school, nor is it to be found in libraries. But they need to know that we were banned from organized baseball by narrow-minded men, and that we played pro ball in a once-thriving league of our own.

They need to know that there were black baseball players the equal of, or better than Babe Ruth, Joe DiMaggio, Cal Ripken, and Mark McGuire. They need to recognize names of stars who made the Hall of Fame—Josh Gibson, Satchel Paige—and those who didn't, but should have—Sam Bankhead, Pee Wee Butts, Wild Bill Wright, Fireball Beverly, and many others.

They need to meet the entrepreneurs, black and some white, who ran the business end. They need to know about the institution that gave a start to players who would come to dominate the Major Leagues—like Willie Mays, Larry Doby, and yes, Jackie Robinson, as well as fantastic players who have faded into history but whom to this day I count among my dearest friends.

In every walk of life you will find people who were in some way connected with Negro League Baseball, whether or not they are aware of it.

My travels and conversations have taught me the problem isn't just lack of information. People also need to know fact from fiction. Plenty of books and documentaries exist—and some have famous players' names on them. But of the ones I've seen, about 95 percent are filled with speculation, errors, and outright lies that smear individuals and fudge numbers. I can tell by reading them that the players didn't write them.

Everybody loves statistics, but back then there was no systematic way to keep track of them. Newspapers in major cities covered our games, but half the places we played didn't even have newspapers, much less sportswriters, and much of what you'll see or read has been cobbled together by people who weren't there.

Some of the films I have seen, even recently, make the stars of black baseball look like fools or hoodlums. For example, the mighty Josh Gibson was portrayed marching down the street behind a minstrel band before a ball game—something he would never be caught dead doing. Gibson and Jackie Robinson have been shown fighting, when in reality, they never played together.

On the other hand, I heard one of our own say he'd stayed at the best hotels, eaten at the best restaurants, and traveled first class. Now, we played in the same league against each other in the same hamlets and cities, and I can assure you we never knew such luxuries. Yet these stories have become myths that people believe and spread.

The purpose of this book is to fill in some of the missing pages from our history textbooks and tell about a way of life about which Americans should feel both proud and sorry. It's a journey that was tragic, but also fantastic, exciting, and fulfilling.

It's tragic because black ballplayers were perceived and treated as second-class citizens, and many never got the chance to prove themselves side by side on the field with their white brothers. Generations of fans missed a chance to see these great players compete.

It's terrific because from 1920 to 1950, Negro League Baseball gave black men the opportunity to play the sport we loved, and formed the backbone of the black social and cultural scenes. At its height, it attracted more spectators than Major League ball and was perhaps the top black business in the nation. And when integration finally came, veterans of the Negro Leagues helped inject new life into a great American pastime.

Why This Book Is Different

What sets this book apart from other sources is that it's *true*. The only way to learn the facts about black ball is to hear it from one who got to live it, eat it, drink it, and suffer doing it. As one of the last surviving Negro League players and current president of the Negro League Baseball Players' Association, and one who has seen pro baseball evolve for seven decades, I believe it is my duty and privilege to tell our story: both the way of life that was lost and the freedom and justice that was gained.

This book is organized in two parts. First, I highlight the history and experiences of my teammates and me during the heyday of the Negro Leagues, giving you the real inside story. Then, I talk about our legacy, which is just as important. That legacy includes our later sports careers, life after baseball in near obscurity, and the slow but sure recognition that has allowed us to take our proper place in society. Throughout, I talk about the friendships formed, which may be the most important thing that came of our experience. Through these bonds, we continue to touch each other's lives—and, we hope, the lives of others, especially children.

So take a seat, and *let's play black ball!*

—Stanley Glenn, December 31, 2005

PART I

What Were the Negro Leagues?

Professional baseball wasn't always about steroid-pumped superstars, multimillion-dollar salaries, and pricey, hard-to-get tickets. Between 60 and 100 years ago, the sport was a humbler form of recreation, played and watched by ordinary folk, and usually run by families or small businesspeople instead of corporate kingpins.

As an enterprise, baseball sometimes struggled to survive. In the 1920s and early 30s, Major League matches were not drawing large crowds. Though attendance perked up a bit after the Great Depression, most teams (except the New York Yankees and maybe the St. Louis Cardinals) had a limited following. Why, in my hometown of Philadelphia, the Athletics and the Phillies were lucky to attract half-a-million people a season. By the time World War II began, the only reason the game was even played was because President Franklin D. Roosevelt thought it would keep up morale. It helped people to have fun and relax.

And while today's fans are now used to seeing African Americans and Latinos on the diamond, "Negroes," as we were called, were unwelcome on Major League teams.

Of course, African Americans have been playing baseball from the time the game was invented in the 1800s. But until all too recently, the country's institutions—businesses, schools, and clubs—were separated by race. It was not just in the South, with its "Jim Crow' segregation laws, but everywhere.

If you were black, there were so many places you simply *could not go*. Why, in Philadelphia there was a six-block area of fine theaters between the main drags on Market and Chestnut streets where we weren't allowed. Even at the neighborhood movie house, there were certain places you had to sit. And if you weren't welcome in Philadelphia venues, don't even think about it in Baltimore or Washington, D.C.! (New York City was always a little bit different, more open-minded. I suppose that was because so many different cultures already mingled there.)

Baseball was no exception to the rule of segregation. As far as I know, there was nothing actually written down saying white Major League teams couldn't hire players who were black, or other people of color. They could have if they'd wanted to, but they didn't. Sports is an old-boys' network, and those old boys had a (usually) unspoken, across-the-board agreement about it.

Of course, there have always been people who favored integrating sports. In fact, in the mid-to-late '40s, some sportswriters started asking Baseball Commissioner Kenesaw Mountain Landis and the team owners *why* there were no black men in Major League Baseball. Can you imagine their answer? *They said we could not play.* That was one of the biggest fallacies ever, and to this day that comment still gets my goat.

In the face of these attitudes, black men with means and drive took it upon themselves to form and run Negro League Baseball, a recognized organization of professional teams that existed between 1920 and 1950. So just as there might be a white entrance and a "colored" entrance to a building, there were two sports organizations: white baseball and black baseball.

But listen: We may have been considered second-class citizens, but we didn't play second-class ball. In spite of the limitations, we worked with what we had, and as much as possible turned disadvantages into advantages.

Take team size, for example. For a long time, the white Major Leagues had 16 teams with, normally, 25 players. The Negro Leagues had only 12 teams carrying 16 players each—17 at most. That meant getting picked was tough, because athletes were scouted and recruited not just from the sandlots, high schools, and colleges of the United States but from Canada and the Latin American countries, too. The only top people excluded were those who were already well off financially, and chose for themselves the more comfortable life of a businessman.

That meant Negro League Baseball players were *the very best there were.* For a number of years during the 1930s and 40s, the main attraction of the Major Leagues was its superstars, big home-run hitters like Babe Ruth and later Ted Williams, and that was about it. But my goodness, in the Negro Leagues we had five guys on *every* team that could hit the ball out of the ballpark!

We played as well as we did because our players were both physically and mentally stronger than their white counterparts. It's because of the world we grew up in. We dealt with the limits and insults of racism every day, and it taught us to be tough. In fact, we often ran faster, threw straighter, powered more home runs, bunted more, lasted longer, and hit for better averages.

Stanley Glenn

Picture it: the joy of catching Satchel Paige, one of baseball's all-time greatest pitchers, with his "bee ball"—a fastball so swift you could hardly see it. Or going to the ballpark knowing a very young Willie Mays is there to play against you, matching his speed with the speed of the baseball, catching doubles and triples and then always throwing the ball to the right base. Or playing the Indianapolis Clowns, where a youthful Hank Aaron, Goose Tatum and others were awaiting your next step. Then, baseball didn't get much better. What fun we had!

In the Negro Leagues, we weren't simply experts at the game. We had a distinct style of play that was faster and more tenacious, with more power and more flair than in Major League Baseball. In fact, many black ball players played the game the *opposite* of white players, hitting, catching the ball, throwing, and running in unorthodox ways.

For the Major Leagues, baseball was a simple base-to-base-to-base game, and frankly a bit boring. They had a lot of rules that we didn't, and in general played more by the book. Pitchers could not throw spitballs, greaseballs, cut balls, or emery balls, and they could put no substance on the block that could be seen. In the Negro Leagues, nobody cared what you put on the ball; you simply went out and pitched. At the end of a day, the pitcher still had to throw a strike! Sure, some of the pitchers were wild intentionally, and sure, somebody might say you threw a spitball at them, but hey—it was going to be dried off by the time they found it.

Another example: 95 percent of the pitchers in our league threw at or very close to most hitters. To get knocked down was just part of the game. However, hitters never charged the mound as they do today. Umpires didn't even warn pitchers for throwing at hitters. The ump would simply tell the hitter to get in there and hit!

We stretched the rules, took a license to be more creative and devious, and used the element of surprise. This made our games more interesting because they were less predictable. Think of what Americans and their children missed, and what white ballplayers missed, because of that: a chance to compete with the top athletes of the era.

Funny thing of it is, not all of our players were even "black." In those times, if you had any blood in you other than Caucasian, you were considered "colored." Some players were so fair they could almost pass, and I'll give you one guess for why: They had a white parent or grandparent who may (or may not) have acknowledged them. Others may have been dark in color, but were actually Latin or another ethnicity.

So when we say "Negro League Baseball," or "the Negro Leagues," that includes our many players from Cuba, Puerto Rico, Venezuela, Maracaibo, Santo Domingo, Mexico and all over Canada. The Philadelphia Stars team alone had three Panamanians on our roster: shortstop Frank

---

OLD TIMERS AND HEYDAY HEROES

Let me introduce you to a few super black baseball players who played before my time, in the old Hilldale Club, predecessor to the Philadelphia Stars.

There was **Smokey Joe Williams**, a big pitcher of that time. He was one of those flame throwers that no one wanted to face, one of the top great pitchers of all time. The home run king of that period was **Louis Santop**, a great catcher who made throws to first base and second base without standing up. Then there was **Mule Suttles**, who could hit it 600 feet, only not often enough. He played first base and the outfield. Turkey **Stearnes** was another player who had everything and loved to play.

As for those fine Negro League players whom I *did* play against, well, there isn't enough room in one book to talk about all of them. So I'll simply name some of the ones who aren't otherwise mentioned here. Many of them played for several different teams, and most have already passed away—but I hope you'll look them up!

Newt Allen, Bud Barbee, Charles Biot, Lyman Bostock, Bob Boyd, Larry Brown, Willard Brown, George Crowe, Jimmy Crutchfield, Doc Dennis, Frank Duncan, Jr., Leroy Ferrell, William Greason, Sam Hairston, Cowan Bubba Hyde, Byron Johnson, Connie Johnson, Josh Johnson, Cecil Kaiser, Larry Kimbrough, Dick Lundy, Red Moore, Willie Pat Patterson, Jim Pendleton, Art Pennington, Nat Pollard, Dave Pope, Charlie Rivera, Bob Romby, Jose Santiago, Dick Seay, Barney Smell, Alvin Spearman, Joe B. Spencer, Jake Stevens, Alfred Surratt, Earl Taborn, Joe Taylor, Bob Telman, Bob Trice, Armando Vasquez, Archie Ware, Cotton Williams, Jesse Williams, Al Wilmore, Bill Yancey, and **Jim Zapp.**

Apologies to anyone I've forgotten, for there are many more beyond memory.

Austin, and outfielders Archie Brathwaite and a guy named Mahoney. Back then, before the revolution of Fidel Castro, Cuba was a U.S. ally, and without question had the best ballplayers I've ever seen. Here, as in many ways, the Major Leagues' loss was the Negro Leagues' gain.

Our History

Minority baseball teams were really nothing new in this country. Serious ball clubs had first started forming in the early 1900s, once African Americans from the South started migrating up to the northern and Midwestern cities, where jobs were more plentiful. However, these clubs had almost no money and weren't very well organized, so they never survived for long. On top of that, there were a lot of team name changes along the way. It's easy to see why good records are hard to come by!

Then along comes a prince of a man by the name of Andrew "Rube" Foster, a former ballplayer himself. Rube was a fearsome pitcher with a mighty arm, known for striking out strings of hitters. He was great enough to join the Majors, but his race prevented that. So he played on black teams whose names faded into history long ago: the Chicago Union Giants, the Cuban X-Giants, and the Philadelphia Giants. Rube later went into management for another team called the Leland Giants.

At the time, white men ran most such teams as well as the Major Leagues. So when he approached the majors to take a look at some of his players, they turned him down. Instead of just accepting the situation, Foster decided it would be better if black baseball was run by African Americans themselves. So in February 1920, he sat down with a group in a Kansas City YMCA and organized eight Midwestern teams into America's first black professional baseball league. It was known as the Negro National League (NNL), and he was its first president.

It's no surprise we now call Rube Foster the Father of Black Baseball. It is because of him that black ballplayers have dominated the sport for more than 50 years.

There are many other forgotten greats—most black, some white—who shared Rube Foster's dream and helped to make that dream a reality.

Edward Bolden is another important name in Negro League History. A postal worker, businessman, and baseball fan from Darby, Pennsylvania, Bolden forged seven other black teams into the Eastern Colored League (ECL) in 1923. The following year, the first of 11 Negro World Series was played between the top teams in the two leagues.

Both the ECL and NNL folded because of money problems—in '28 and '31, respectively. That was just a bump in the road, though: independent teams continued to compete against each other. Of course, the road was pretty bumpy: New leagues would get started, like the American Negro League, East-West League, and Negro Southern League, only to fold after a short while.

Also in 1931, a wealthy black entrepreneur and nightclub owner named Gus Greenlee stepped into the picture. Greenlee had recently bought the legendary Pittsburgh Crawfords, a baseball team with one of the best rosters ever assembled. The lineup included five future Hall of Famers: Satchel Paige, Cool Papa Bell, Josh Gibson, William "Judy" Johnson, and Oscar Charleston. (I'll talk more about each of them later.)

Gus didn't like the fact that his players weren't allowed to use the locker rooms in white-owned ballparks, so he took it upon himself to build a stadium especially for the Crawfords and other black teams. Set up in the hills of Pittsburgh, Greenlee Field was the first black-owned major baseball field in America.

Greenlee's ball club, field, and restaurants were legitimate businesses, but a lot of his wealth came from the underground practice of numbers running. He was no gangster, though. The numbers game was a sort of street lottery, similar to off-track betting. It was like running speakeasies during Prohibition—not legal, but everybody did it anyway. At that time, the numbers business was a great thing for many black folk. It paid out when people hit, and there was no rowdiness that I know of connected to it.

Two years later, Greenlee revived and ran the Negro National League and organized the first Negro League All-Star game. For a while, the NNL was the only pro black baseball league, and most of the teams were from the East Coast.

The team I wound up joining, the Philadelphia Stars, was also started in 1933. It originated from the old Hilldale club, one of the top teams in early Negro League Baseball during the teens and 1920s. Based in the Philadelphia suburb of Darby, the team (then called the Daisies) had won three championships in the old ECL and triumphed in the 1925 Negro World Series.

Hilldale existed thanks to the partnership of Edward Bolden and John Drew. Bolden, of course, also helped start the Eastern league, and Drew was the owner of the DTC Transportation Company, a bus line similar to today's SEPTA. Bolden and Drew had a falling out for some reason, and Hilldale eventually folded. But Bolden was eager to start another team and bring it up to big-league stature.

As a civil servant, his funds were low, so he arranged for backing from a white man named Eddie Gottlieb, a very successful and well-known Philly sports promoter, and moved the team to the city. The Philadelphia Stars' first season was 1934, and they won the Negro National League pennant that same year!

Then in 1937, J.L. Wilkinson, the owner of a team called the Kansas City Monarchs, organized several southern and midwestern teams together into the Negro American League. Like Gottlieb, Wilkinson was one of the few white men in sports without an ounce of racism in him. Both were assets to Negro League Baseball.

Now there were two stable leagues, composed of 12 teams: the NNL, known as the East, and the NAL, called the West. ("West" was relative: Some NAL teams were actually of the South, and the furthest west was in Kansas City.)

The six teams of the NNL were the New York Cubans, the New York Black Yankees, the Newark Eagles, The Philadelphia Stars, the Baltimore Elite Giants, and the Homestead Grays (of Pittsburgh, and later Washington, D.C.).

The six teams of the NAL were the Kansas City Monarchs, the Chicago American Giants, the Indianapolis Clowns, the Cleveland Buckeyes, the Memphis Red Sox, and the Birmingham Black Barons.

Some teams were better than others, but each had its share of phenomenal players. Some of these guys you've probably heard of, but I knew them at another level. Others you might call unsung heroes. Quite a few became my good friends off the field for a long time—even a lifetime.

Mind you, many if not most people played for several different teams during their Negro League careers. Just like in Major League ball, the teams would trade players. At the time, neither Negro League nor Major League players had any say about which team they played for or for how long. The owners would decide to trade you, rehire you, or fire you at will.

(For those who want to dig deeper into detail about the teams, their players and owners, and their particular traits, look in the boxes with dark borders scattered through this book. Most of what I recall here was who they were with during most of *my* time. Of course, I remember the most detail about the teams of the East, because that was my league. Also, the Philadelphia Stars played against them more often.)

Anyway, outside of the race and flamboyance of our players, Negro League Baseball was just that: professional baseball. We used regular bats, gloves, uniforms, and bases, and played the usual positions on normal diamonds. Our organization had the same type of officials in charge, the same seasons, and so forth. (Our spring training started a few weeks later than theirs did though.)

We also played everywhere the majors did: in Yankee Stadium and the Polo Grounds in New York City, Ebbet's Field and Bushwicks in Brooklyn, Ruppert Stadium in Newark, Shibe Park in Philadelphia, Forbes Field in Pittsburgh, Bugle Field in Baltimore, Griffith Stadium in Washington, D.C., Bugle Triple A Stadium in Indianapolis, Comiskey Park in Chicago, and the Triple A parks in Birmingham, Alabama and Kansas City, Missouri. Those are some of the most exciting games I remember.

We were able to do this because booking agents like Eddie Gottlieb arranged

to rent the parks for us when the Majors didn't need them—like when they were playing an out-of-town game. The Major League teams didn't really care if black teams used their stadiums if they weren't in them. And when the owners saw the chance to make an extra dollar, they put their prejudices aside.

The Negro League teams played one another in regularly scheduled games, just like in Major League baseball. Inter-league play was also commonplace back then. (Now, *that* was unheard of in the Majors until much later, save for their World Series and All Star games. I have no idea why, other than that they finally realized the practice was more competitive.)

For a while, Negro League teams sometimes even played exhibition games against white Major League teams. That is, until Baseball Commissioner Kenesaw Mountain Landis put a stop to it. In the early 1930s after one of the World Series between the Philadelphia Athletics and the St. Louis Cardinals, someone arranged for the old Hilldale team to play the Athletics at the ballpark near Darby, Pennsylvania. Well, Hilldale beat the Athletes so badly that Landis chewed them out for letting "niggers" defeat them. And he declared that no more intact white teams would be allowed to play black teams again. Especially after they'd just played in the series, he thought it made them look bad and had to be stopped. Obviously, his doing that further divided the worlds of black and white pro baseball.

Like I said, the Negro Leagues had their own annual World Series and All Star games. The Series was between the NNL league champion team and the NAL champion team, with the winner best four out of seven. The East-West All-Star game was between the best players of the NNL and the best of the NAL. Both contests were played in the daytime rather than at night, so children as well as their parents could watch them. The East-West game, held in Chicago's Comiskey Park, attracted huge crowds. We were that popular, even without the Fan Fests and other promotions as they have today.

Besides playing in all those fine ballparks, we also did something the Majors *didn't* do: We barnstormed, traveling from town to town across America and making pit stops to play local teams (both black and white) in hamlets and towns where people had to stand to watch.

All we wanted to do was play baseball, anytime, anywhere. And from New York to California and Canada down to Texas, if there was some semblance of a baseball field, I don't know any place in America where one of us *didn't* play. We often played three games in one day, and some teams played four. We had a following wherever we went. It is for sure we traveled too much, but the experiences we had and the people we met made it worth the trouble.

All told, the Negro Leagues were in their glory for three decades. Truly, it was a magnificent time to live and play baseball. The players seldom talked of racism or even going to the big leagues. We felt we *were* the big leagues.

Growing Up with the Negro Leagues

I've borne witness to Negro League history, and played my own part in it. And I suppose I'm as good an example as anyone of a typical player. So we may as well begin by getting you acquainted with the guy who's writing this book.

I, Stanley Glenn, was born on September 19, 1926, the fourth living child of Charles and Lorenda Glenn. Home was on the southeastern Shore of Virginia in the village of Wachapreague, a deep-sea-fishing town on the Chesapeake Bay.

My father was a fisherman who'd lived there all his life. My mother hailed from the shores of Maryland, and worked in the fish houses where they process oysters, clams, and shrimp. She went only as far as the third grade, and my father went to the fourth grade. Yet they were two of the smartest and wisest people I've ever known in my life. In the Glenn household, there was never talk of hatred no matter what the situation was. Dad and Mom preached love to their children and in turn I preached love to mine.

My father was a straight-up guy. He never promised to punish you: If you had a beating coming you were going to get it right then and there. I thanked him and loved him for that. Mom was the homemaker who did the cooking and caring and all the things that moms do. You didn't get promises from her either. We kids believed that whatever Mom and Dad said was law.

We were poor as sin, but happy. We grew our own vegetables in a garden and also raised pigs. All of our other food we got from the ocean. I was the baby of the family and learned to fish when I was only five years old. The sea must be in my blood, because I still love to fish.

My mother had four sisters and two brothers, and all of them lived along the coast. Our extended clan did just about everything social together, as many black families had to do back then—we didn't have the money to do anything else!

We had to make our own pleasure. Picnics, cookouts, and outings were a great pastime, because they were cheap and you didn't have to travel far to enjoy them. The church was also an important part of life, both spiritually and socially. It was a place where nice people met and married their spouses, a place where we were taught no hate, and where peace and harmony reigned. It was one of the few places where we were truly free.

All in all, Wachapreague was a quiet, classic Southern town. Residents were very proud people, every one of them baseball lovers. Why, on Saturday afternoons people came from miles around to see the locals play ball. All families played it, and played it well: fathers and mothers, sisters and brothers, uncles and aunts. A team or two of kids was a neighborhood staple.

Playing and watching baseball united black Americans at a time when other options were limited. Though people now think of basketball and football as the domain of black athletes, those sports didn't really get integrated until the late 1950s and early '60s. Yes, baseball was our game, for both amateurs and professionals.

True to tradition, my father and brother Robert played baseball before me, and I'd started playing myself by the time I was in the third grade. Robert, who was 12 years older than me, was a catcher, so of course I had to be a catcher, too. Some said he was a better one than me. That was all right, because he was family.

Until I was about 10 years old, I was a terrible kid. I was mischievous and just plain ornery. I took after my father's father, who was so obnoxious that when he asked my parents to name me after him, they flat out refused! Once, when I was supposed to be asleep I heard my mom and dad praying aloud that God would save me.

By then, my family had moved to Philadelphia. A couple of years before, Betty, one of my married sisters, had come down with her new baby to Wachapreague to visit for a month. Just as she was ready to go back home, we were all sitting out on the porch and my father turned to my mother and said, "Renda, don't you think it's time *we* moved to the city?" They wanted to be near their grandchildren.

The next thing I knew, we were living out near the Philadelphia airport, on Holstein Avenue in a two-story semi-detached house. We then moved a couple more times around Southwest Philly, finally settling in a huge duplex on 58th St. and Baltimore Avenue that had five rooms and a bath on each floor.

That wound up suiting me fine, because Pennsylvania was a mecca for baseball. Plenty of the most famous names in pro baseball, both black and white, have been natives of Pittsburgh or Philadelphia. There's Roy Campanella, Stan Musial, Carl Furillo, and Pete Suter, to name but a few.

Locally, we had the all-white Phillies and the Athletics teams, but since they weren't interested in hiring anyone from Philadelphia's black community, we weren't exactly their fans. Naturally, we preferred the Negro Leagues teams, the Philadelphia Stars and Pittsburgh's Homestead Grays.

Philadelphia was some town in those days. The population then was some 3 million strong, twice what it is now. Manufacturing and the military were thriving. Wherever in the city you traveled, it seemed that every home, apartment, and business was occupied, a far cry from the abandoned buildings you see today. Numerous city newspapers were published—including three black papers, the *Independent,* the *Courier*, and the *Tribune*, which still exists. So there were always several sportswriters around to cover the city's black baseball games.

Black men from all over the region and up from the South would come to Philadelphia to take jobs in manufacturing, and play in what were known as the Industrial Leagues. Westinghouse, General Electric, Baldwin Locomotives (now Boeing), General Steel, and all of the area Navy yards each had a baseball league, so a man could work full time to support himself and his family and also play on the company team. They had some fine athletes; I daresay some employers would give a guy a job *just* to play the sport. If a company possessed a star player, that was a feather in its cap. That was important in a big baseball town.

Sometimes professional baseball teams recruited from the Industrial Leagues. And sometimes they'd get turned down because the worker/players were already making out well—4,500–$5,000 a year to hold a job and play ball. In the '40s, that would practically make you a millionaire.

Since baseball was so important to our community, it's no surprise that in Philadelphia and all across America, for six months of each year, Negro League Baseball was a main attraction among African Americans of all ages.

Going to a game was affordable, even for the best seats. A box cost about a dollar-fifty, whereas today it might set you back thousands of dollars. They had rows of bleachers where us kids could come sit and watch on a Saturday afternoon. It was also convenient: In Philadelphia, for example, the trolley car went right by the door of the ballpark, and you could transfer to or from the subway, all for 15 cents.

THE HOMESTEAD GRAYS

The **Homestead Grays**, based in Pittsburgh, Pennsylvania and playing in Forbes Field and Washington, D.C.'s Griffith Stadium, were probably the best and most powerful team put together in the 1940s. They could beat you many ways.

For one thing, the Grays got all of the legendary players that used to play for Gus Greenlee's semi-unbeatable Pittsburgh Crawfords after they went out of business—outfielder Cool Papa Bell, catcher Josh Gibson, and first baseman Buck Leonard. No surprise the Grays went on to win nine consecutive NNL pennants. **James "Cool Papa" Bell** had legs—he was a real base-stealer who could probably outrun a cheetah. **Buck Leonard**, first baseman, was the consummate hitter, fielder, base runner, and leader by example.

Then there was **Josh Gibson**. Baseball has all kinds of stories, and many of them have yeast in them, but you can believe the stories about Josh. He was one of the first players who did not play in the Major Leagues who made the Hall of Fame. And if they had not put him in there, they might as well demolish the whole thing!

For one thing, Josh Gibson hit more home runs than anyone who played the game. Let me tell you, he was the best right-handed hitter I have ever seen. When you fooled Josh, and that was seldom, he still hit the ball 400 feet. When he was at bat, even the infielders moved into the outfield! Josh was so feared as a hitter that when he played in Mexico they made him a lead-off hitter and walked him leading off the game.

What's more, he could also run well for a big man (he was about 6'2" and 235 lbs). I remember him as a fun-loving guy—until the time he hit me in a collision at the plate in Griffith Stadium. I actually went numb and forgot where I was. That taught me a lesson I never forgot. Josh had shortcomings, but they were not on the ballfield.

Tragically, Josh died of a stroke at age 36. It was 1947, and we were playing winter ball in Caracas, Venezuela. A telegram came for **Sam Bankhead**, who was acting as manager down there, saying that Josh had died. Well, Sam went ballistic with grief. We had to hold him down and finally had to put him in the hospital. He and Josh had been roommates for years, and they were like brothers. I don't think he was ever the same afterwards.

It's actually a toss-up as to who among those three created the most interest, but let me tell you they created havoc: Josh and Buck Leonard with their long balls, and Cool with his speed and the ability to hit ground balls and turn them into singles and doubles. Too numerous times Josh or Buck didn't even have to get a hit—they had only to make contact, then it was case closed.

The team had many other great players. There was **Wilmer Fields** in the outfield or at third base, or pitching and hitting with power. Off the field he was a truly fine man and a caring friend. **Jerry Benjamin** was a stellar centerfielder with great speed and a great contact hitter. Sam Bankhead at shortstop was the brains of this team, a very steady fielder who never made a bad throw. When a key hit was needed, Sam produced. Sam was such a great relay man, he took all throws from the outfield because it would be a strike to whatever base. You don't usually hear much about Sam, but he was something.

In seven seasons I never saw Sam make a bad throw from shortstop or as the relay man. Sam was to the Grays what Pee Wee Reese and Jackie Robinson were to the Dodgers. He was not spectacular unless you know the finer parts of playing. Sam was probably a .250 or .260 hitter, but that one-for-four almost always resulted in a run batted in.

One of the old timers on the Grays was **Boojum Wilson**, a strong left-handed hitter and third baseman whose chest was made of steel. If he did not field the ball, he played it off his chest, and he still made the play. There was another great catcher on the team named **Rob Roy Gaston**. After Josh died, Rob took over as first-string catcher, and made sure the catching did not suffer.

Luke Easter was a left-handed hitter who hit home runs to left field like a strong right-handed hitter. Very seldom did Luke hit the ball to the right side of the diamond. He was the size of Sherman Tank, about 6' 7" or 6' 8" without an ounce of fat.

The pitching stall was top-notch, too, with **Ray Brown, Garnet Blair, Roy Wellmaker, Edsal Walker, Cecil Kaiser, Tom Parker, Spoon Carter**, and **Roy Parttow.**

The manager of this great group was **Candy Jim Taylor**, who was old and ill, but loved the game. After Candy Jim came **Vic Harris**, able and intelligent. They were excellent baseball men who loved challenging games—definitely the right guys for the job.

The Grays' owner was an important figure, **Cumberland "Cum" Posey**. A real baseball man, he was the guy who'd started the East-West League in the '30s, which didn't last. From about 1912 on, he played for and then managed the team, and finally bought it from Gus Greenlee. He was involved for more than three decades, till the end. Cum traveled with his team all the time, even when he was getting on in years. Anyone who can handle that at an advanced age has got to be kind of special!

More than that, though, Negro League Baseball was *THE* thing—a happening, a way of life. Everybody loved the sport. Back then, watching a baseball game was a celebration. Women and men came to the ballpark dolled up in their finest. Ladies wore dresses, long-sleeved gloves, silk stockings, and high-heeled shoes. Each gal was trying to out-dress the others; one would have thought it was a national fashion show. My goodness, it could be 90 degrees out, and a woman would be sitting there with her back just as straight as could be, and the men were the same. They'd come to the ballpark in shirts and ties, shoes shined, looking for women to woo. Yes, if you wanted to date and mate, this was the place because that's where everyone went to see and be seen.

The times generally were more formal and polite. Ladies, gentlemen, and children always wore a hat when they went out. And you didn't see people at the ballpark in shorts or dungarees—that was for the beach.

You got the occasional rowdiness, but that's universal at sports events, especially when beer and booze are sold. But if you got put out for misbehaving, you weren't allowed back. Negro League games had the same police protection as the Major League teams; the cops were civil servants paid to keep the peace no matter who was using the ballpark.

Not surprisingly, before I had even reached my teens I was playing baseball in earnest. I loved the game, and I was determined to be a catcher like my brother Robert—so I could be better than him! We kids would form our own leagues in the city's neighborhoods and had a lot of fun.

In my neighborhood of southwest Philadelphia, most people didn't have cars, and we kids didn't have trolley fare (we saved what coins we had for movies on the weekends). So we walked, ran, or biked everywhere, and it made us fit and fast. I myself walked four miles up and back each day when I was in junior high and high school. It didn't matter if it was raining or the snow was two feet deep. In fact, unlike kids of today who watch TV all day long and get no exercise, we spent more time playing baseball than watching it.

One reason for that was, for a kid, it was too far to go to see a game unless you were willing to make a whole day of it. But when the regular World Series came around town, I played hooky from school so I could see the games, which were played during the daylight hours. (Though the teams were segregated, anyone could be a spectator.) Of course, I watched Negro League games live, too, when I could get to them. Naturally I rooted for my home team, the Philadelphia Stars.

I did my share of watching Major League Baseball games on screen, as well. I liked the St. Louis Cardinals because they played a fast, tough game. They were always running over people. I didn't like the Yankees or the Red Sox so much, because they hit home runs and it just wasn't challenging enough.

By the time I got to John Bartram High School in February of 1942, not long after World War II began, I was 6'2" and weighed about 190 pounds. At the time, only a few black students played sports. But the coach at Bartram, a fine man named Emmanuel "Menschy" Goldblatt, gave me and my buddy James "Chip" Wilkes our chance to play with the Clippers, the school's baseball team. He got instant results. Our second year, our team won the public league championship, and tied for the title the following year.

Menschy was a no-nonsense coach and also insisted your grades be good or you could not play ball for him. Thankfully I'd always been a good student so I had no problem there. The rule held on the field, too: You goofed up, and boy, you were going to get it. Fortunately, I was one of the best players on the team and Mr. Goldblatt brought out the best in me.

Over time, Menschy became more than a coach: He was a mentor. He'd graduated from the University of Pennsylvania when it was almost unheard of for a Jewish boy to be accepted at an Ivy League school. So he knew a little bit about being an outsider. Over time, we grew so close he became like a second father to me. I got to know his entire family well, and we stayed in touch after I finished school.

Years later, after Chip Wilkes had gone on to the Newark Eagles and I'd gone on to the Philadelphia Stars, our team used to play in the field at 44th Street and Parkside Avenue. Sometimes, in the middle of a game, I'd look up and Coach Goldblatt would be standing in the stands, watching and wondering how I was doing.)

THE NEWARK EAGLES

The **Newark Eagles** were a bunch of free-swinging long-ball hitters with finesse and know-how. They were definitely one of the best teams in the leagues, particularly in 1946. That year, there were five fellows in that ballclub who are now in the Hall of Fame in Cooperstown, New York: Larry Doby, Monte Irvin, Ray Dandridge, Leon Day, and Willie Wells. No surprise they won our World Series that year.

Len Pearson, a first baseman and a power hitter, had bad legs but could steal a base when needed. He played hard, lived hard, and was the fourth-place hitter on a team of ball busters.

Then there was **Larry Doby**, later the first black player in the American League. No second baseman who ever lived had Doby's force. He was not a big guy, but was very, very powerful. Personally, he was a very quiet person, almost an introvert, who tended to keep to himself, though I got to know him well.

The world's second-best third baseman (after Judy Johnson) was **Raymond Dandridge**, an accurate thrower and a line-drive hitter with good speed who didn't believe anyone could hit the ball past him. Danny, as we affectionately called him, did not remember anyone by name, but knew very well what you did on the field.

Willie Wells was the shortstop; he always threw out the base runner by one step, and could really play. **Johnny Davis**, who was part Indian, was a left fielder with great power and was a real guess hitter. No one hit the ball harder, except maybe Josh Gibson. Then there was **Monte Irvin**, a talented infielder and out-fielder with good power. **Bob Harvey**, an outfielder, was a good hitter, fair fielder, and a good team man.

Jimmie 'Chip" Wilkes, one of baseball's great centerfielders, was small in size but wielded power when he wanted to or needed an extra bit. We have been friends since elementary school, and I was disappointed when we wound up play-ing on different teams. His parents and mine were also close.

Newark had some fine pitchers, led by one of my personal favorites, the one and only **Leon Day**, who many say was Satchel Paige's equal. In fact, his record shows that out of 13 times he faced Satchel, he actually won several of those games. There was no other quite like Leon. He was mean as a rattlesnake on the mound, a power pitcher with excellent control. He was wild when he wanted to be wild, and threw strikes when he wanted to throw strikes. Leon could also play a great second base and outfield, and was a line-drive hitter.

Don Newcombe, or Nuke, as we called him, was a power pitcher. Then there was bad, bald **Terris McDuffie**, in my estimation the best I ever faced anywhere, and **Len Hooker** and **Warren Peace**, both junk ballers.

I've saved one of the best for last: **Max Manning**. Max, long and lean, was a side-armed pitcher like Ewell Blackwell of Cincinnati fame. Max knew what he was doing out there. What's more, he was a complete gentleman; we were very close even though we didn't play on the same team. He deserves to be in the Hall of Fame.

Somebody else who should be in the Hall of Fame was **Raleigh "Biz" Mackey**, their catcher, manager, and also a teacher, and developer. He goes all the way back to the Hilldale Club. A big, jovial guy, Biz really loved the game and was probably baseball's best catcher. He was a super handler of pitches and a clutch hitter in his old days, and taught Roy Campanella how to catch and to take com-mand of his pitching staff. In fact, if you'd ever watched Campanella catch, you'd see the Mackey in him. In 1945 he was 48 years old, and still managing and catching every day. "Cali," as we called him because he lived in California, was never too busy or occupied to talk baseball.

The Eagles were owned by **Abe Manley**, who was also in the numbers-running business, and his wife, **Effa Manley**, who really ran the show. Both of them were deeply involved in administration of the league: Abe was VP and treasurer of the NNL for a while, and Effa was its secretary. Boy, Effa was something. So fair-skinned you could almost mistake her for white, she was gorgeous and looked like a movie star. But Effa was a tough lady who dealt eye-to-eye with all the men in the sports and business worlds. She could do anything!

I played baseball during the summers and in season during the school year. The rest of the time, September to Easter, I worked a part-time job delivering kerosene for Ace Oil Company. I'd get out of school about 2 p.m., call up my boss, Mr. Baker, and see what he had for me to do. That job sometimes kept me busy six days a week, sunup to sundown. It kept money in my pocket, so I could contribute to my household. It also kept me out of trouble!

Sometimes, though, my friends and I would sneak into Shibe Park, the Major League stadium, to watch the Philadelphia Athletics practice before a night game. I thought Frankie Hayes, one of the Athletics' catchers, was quite good, and over time I got to know him.

One day Frankie taught me how to catch a pop-up in five minutes. He was taking a little break and decided to coach me, probably because he knew I was also a catcher. I mentioned that I was having trouble catching pop-ups. "I can do it," I said, "but I don't look good at it. I'm stumbling all over myself."

He said, "Sonny, when the ball goes straight up over your head, don't move. Wait until it gets up there and comes back down. Make eye contact, and when the ball feels like it's going to *hit you right in the nose*, it'll be a foot in front of you. *Then* catch it!"

(That advice really helped, and I continued to follow Hayes after he stopped playing professionally and joined a little semi-pro team down in Point Pleasant, New Jersey. By that point I'd joined the Stars, and our team would play them once or twice a year. Frankie was getting old by then, so he didn't want to catch. One time, he was playing first base and missed a couple of balls. "That's it!" he said. "Next inning, I'm catching!")

Between Menschy and Frankie and just playing, I continued to improve my game. Well, when you're a good player in high school, word gets around, and pro teams always have their scouts on the lookout for the next big thing. And in 1943, something very special happened to me—and more than likely I'm not the only young black athlete it happened to. I was almost recruited by the New York Yankees.

Apparently the Yankees' coach, Art Fletcher, heard tell about the Clippers' hot pitcher—me! So one day he and his associates made a trip down to Bartram High School to watch me play. But first they dropped in at the school office to talk to Coach Goldblatt. He told them, "I can bring Stan down here but I don't really want to." Fletcher asked why and he replied simply, "He's a black guy." Fletcher didn't say another word. He walked out, got in his car, and drove back to New York.

Coach Goldblatt did not have the heart to tell me about the incident. I heard rumors a few weeks later from some teammates hanging around the gym office. But I didn't really believe it, and frankly, I didn't care. All I wanted to do was play ball, and I didn't care where or who for.

THE NEW YORK CUBANS

These guys could beat you with speed, power, pitching, and great defense. They played in the Polo Grounds, to crowds of more than 30,000.

The **New York Cubans** had its greats; most (but not all) of its players were from the Latin countries. Let's begin with the super **Martin Dihigo**, who played seven positions with precision, finesse, speed, power, and great desire, and could have made the All-Star team at any of them. I am sorry I did not play with or against him, but from all I have heard from really gifted people, Martin was every bit the complete player. He played with such abandon that he often surprised himself. Laughter was present in his demeanor and complete joy was his. All he wanted to do was play: which position or where meant next to nothing to him. He was a marvel who eventually made the Hall of Fame.

Then there was **David "Showboat" Thomas**, considered one of the finest first basemen ever, who also played outfield and managed; infielder **Silvio Garcia**, a Cuban with a high batting average; Wonderful **Horacio Martinez**, a fine shortstop; **"Minnie" Minoso**, a third baseman who played in two Negro League All-Star games and was picked up by the majors early, and had a long career with several teams; and **Pedro Diaz**, a terrific shortstop and catcher.

On the pitching side there was **Dave "Impo" Barnhill**, a little guy who once out-pitched Satchel Paige in our East-West game; **Jose Santiago** from Puerto Rico, an All Star in '48; and **Patricio "Pat" Scantlebury**, a left-handed pitcher who went on to the Cincinnati Reds. **Louis Tiant, Sr.**, was a left-handed pitcher, and would become father to Luis Tiant, Jr, the Boston Red Sox star. Tiant Sr. had the best move to first base I've ever seen, holding runners close. The Cubans' impressive catchers included three-time All Star **Louie Louden**, and **Rafael "Ray" Noble**, who later joined the New York Giants.

The team was owned by a black Cuban named **Alex Pompez**, a former numbers racket man from Harlem. He owned and promoted several black baseball teams during the heyday of Negro League Baseball, and also served as vice president of the NNL. Eventually he became a scout for the New York Giants and worked with the Hall of Fame committee to select players from Negro Leagues.

A few months later, I *was* playing professional baseball beside legendary players in the Negro National League. You see, the Yankees weren't the only ones watching us play. The Clippers played all 11 public schools in the city of Philadelphia. And of course if you're pretty good, before you know it, everybody knows who you are.

One day Oscar Charleston, the manager of the Philadelphia Stars, was scoping out the local teams that played at the Bartram Athletic Field at 58th Street and Elmwood Avenue. Well, the 1944 pro baseball season ended the first week in June, I graduated from Bartram High a week later and a week after that

Charleston signed me to the Stars as a catcher for $175 a month. It was a far cry from the $8 a week I used to earn working for Mr. Baker delivering kerosene. And I was all of 17 years old!

Philadelphia Glory Days

Having success at what one is trying to do at such a young age is quite a thrill. All the seasons I played were special, but 1944 will stand out because I was just a kid and playing with the big boys. I'd never really had a chance to grow up. And let me tell you, my head grew two sizes too big. That's pretty natural: Being hired by the Philadelphia Stars meant I was the cream of the crop.

However, in a very short time, our great leadership, the other players, and the challenges of the game erased my ego.

Ed Bolden was our boss, so we used to call him "Chief." A very quiet man, he was well liked by everyone on the team. Mr. Bolden was the one I would sit down with at the beginning or end of each year to negotiate my contract. Like all Negro League ballplayers agreements, it was modeled on the ones Major League players signed—eventually they'd match them nearly word for word. The form covered annual salary, when to report for spring training, and the schedule of the important weekend games (and sometimes the weekday ones, though we might not know that ahead of time).

In those days before powerful sports unions and collective bargaining, every player had to do his own deal with the team owner the best he could. That was true whether you were in the regular Major Leagues or the Negro Leagues. It was no fortune in either case. The Major League salary at that time was about $5,000 a year. The top pay was barely five figures, and only the really good players made that. As for us, the average salary in the Negro League was from $350 a month up to probably a thousand a month earned by the very best players. We lived on it, so I suppose it was enough. Overall, at least in my experience, business dealings with our bosses seemed fair.

Our manager was Oscar Charleston, a former Stars centerfielder who'd also played for Hilldale and other teams. As my manager and coach for seven seasons, he gave me no rest. He also became a good friend.

In fact, there aren't enough superlatives to describe Charlie, as he was called. In his time, he was probably the equal of Willie Mays, but with more consistency. He had speed, abundant power, and unmatched throwing for many seasons. Centerfield belonged to Charlie. Right center and left center were his also because he caught all triples and made all doubles into singles. He would go on to make the Hall of Fame, and rightfully so. Then he became a manager of the legendary Pittsburgh Crawfords. Managing is one of the toughest jobs in baseball, and was quite successful at it.

As a leader, Charlie had a heart that was unmatched and met challenges on and off the field. His demeanor was such that all players respected it. But he was a little crazy, too—he had a reputation as a hothead, and I sometimes thought that if given half a chance, Charlie would rather fight than play. All in all, he was a no-nonsense guy, but gentle, kind, and understanding as long as you behaved like a professional.

Our booking agent and promoter, Eddie Gottlieb, was a real mover and shaker. We affectionately called him "The Mogul." My high school baseball coach, Menschy Goldblatt, knew Eddie from way back, so when I signed on with the Stars in 1944, he'd already heard about me.

Mr. Gottlieb handled business for all the teams that came into the area. He had a way of getting Negro League teams into Major League ballparks, putting the money up so we could play in places like Yankee Stadium and the Polo Grounds. As far as I know, he was a gentleman and not involved in any illegal enterprises.

Over time, we also became good friends. And when he died in the late 1970s, I actually took a day off work to attend his funeral, like everyone who was anyone from the sports world. We wanted to send him off right.

When I signed on, I was already acquainted with some of my teammates because all the other guys who'd played for the city's high school teams knew one another. Mahlon Duckett, for example, had played for Overbrook High School in West Philadelphia, and Wilmer Harris, who was three years my senior, had played for Central High up in the Olney neighborhood.

Mahlon Duckett

THE PHILADELPHIA STARS

The **Philadelphia Stars** had an aggregation of ballplayers, not only from all over America but also from Latin America. There were many standouts at various points in my career with the team (1944–1950).

We had a fine infield made up of **Shifty Jim West** at first base, a good power hitter and a defensive gem. He was the fourth-place hitter on the team, and knocked in most of the runs. **Marvin Williams**, a small, rangy guy from Conroe, Texas, was a power-hitting second baseman who played with us for a few years. Good old **Mahlon Duckett** was a clutch hitter at second and third base with few superiors anywhere. I thought third base was his best position.

At shortstop, Panamanian **Frank "Junior" Austin** threw a hundred-hitter—he had great range and was a fine lead-off hitter. Ring Ring, as we called him, not only made all the plays a shortstop could make, but could steal bases and keep the whole team loose with his nutty antics. **Bus Clarkson** was also a shortstop, but was moved to third base because Austin played short only. Bus was a good hitter with excellent power and also a good base runner. He was knock-kneed, so we called him "Knocky."

Gene Benson, at center field, was one of the best, a good base runner and second-place hitter who was sure-handed and hit all pitching. Gene invented the basket catch, where he'd catch the ball around his waist; when Willie Mays later came in the league, he too started catching the ball like Benson did. Benson was probably baseball's best center fielder. He had a good shot at the Hall of Fame, though for some reason he never made it, and stayed many years with the Stars. Another fine addition was **Harry Simpson**, an outfielder and a good hitter with speed.

The catching was manned by **Bill Cash** and a guy named **Stanley Glenn**. Bill had the strongest throwing arm of any catcher I've ever seen. Me, I was a hard-nosed strategist who lived and died on the unexpected.

Frank Austin, Gene Benson, and Marvin Williams were all .300 hitters, Jim West and Bus Clarkson were good power hitters, Mahlon Duckett was a clutch hitter, Bill Cash and I had good power, and Harry Simpson had both power and consistency. We also had **Red Parnell**, a great hitter and base runner supreme, and **Henry "Splo" Spearman**, a power hitter. Let's face it: with so many good hitters, the Philadelphia Stars could score runs.

And that was just the offense. When it came to defense, we were leaders. My role as catcher was managing the staff of pitchers, which was quite a privilege because ours were some of the best ever assembled:

Bill Ricks was a power pitcher with excellent curve and change-up. I really loved it when he pitched against the Baltimore Elites. He would tell us before the game that he was going to saw off Roy Campanella's bat in his hands.

Wilmer Harris was a curveball pitcher with a hard sinker ball and two curve balls. He had the best curveball I ever saw. I had great success with his sinker. Wilmer would tell Len Pearson, **Johnny Davis**, and Monte Irvin of the Newark

Eagles that his jugs were ready. He would knock them down and then throw three curveball strikes.

Then there was **Henry Miller**, a power pitcher whose balls were very heavy. A live sinker and slider, Henry had a special way of throwing the ball. He actually *slung* it, side arm and three-quarter, and even he did not know where it was going. Hitters did not want to face him. We were roommates and got along well.

Joe Filmore, who was about 6' 6", could break in a catcher's mitt warming up. His only mistake was if someone got a hit, the next pitch would founder without good direction. He was one of those 98-mph pitchers.

Henry McHenry threw hard. Mac had good knuckle balls, curve balls, crinkle balls, and a good fastball. **Hubert "Country" Glenn** (no relation to me) loved to turn his back to the hitter before delivering the pitch. **Harold Gould** had hard curve balls, good control, a real live fastball, and was in good shape.

Barney Brown, a left-handed pitcher, was my personal favorite. He had five different pitches and could throw strikes with all of them. Barney on his best play had an 80–85 mph fastball. He was a little guy, and much older than me. He knew his craft. Yet, and I don't say this begrudgingly, Barney couldn't write his name. Never mind: He knew what he was going to do, and sometimes he would say to me, "I know so and so is a breaking-ball hitter, but I'm going to throw him my breaking ball!"

Then there was a left-handed pitcher named **Bob Boone** who I didn't much like, as much as I tried to. He didn't have it, as far as I was concerned, or rather, he was decent, but not as good as he thought he was, so we had our disagreements.

They and some of the other players were friendly right away. Others let me know I wasn't wanted. I never will forget an incident up at Yankee Stadium that first year. Bill Cash, who's some eight years my senior, met me at the top of the dugout steps, and declared, "You're going to have to out-catch me, out-hit me, and out-throw me to be the first-string catcher on this team." I paid him no mind. I was just doing my job and I believe he was jealous because I was doing it well and all the pitchers wanted me to catch for them. (By the way, Bill and I are on good terms now!)

I found that after a new player had paid his dues and his game showed that he belonged, then most of his teammates would get on board and make him feel like part of the team. And as I went along, the older players mentored me and other rookies, introducing us to the ones who'd been in the league for a long time and giving advice on which opposing players did what, when, and how we should handle them. In time, I became a very fine catcher and hit with power.

But first, there was a lot to learn. In Negro League Baseball, there was no farm system to develop promising new players. It was more like on-the-job training. On day one you reported for spring training, and on day two you proved yourself and played a game. (That was OK, because for my own first 10 years in pro ball, I felt that I didn't really need any training: I was young, fit, and a little on the crazy side.)

Then there was the challenge of playing on a real small team—only 16 men. For one thing, there were few relief players. So like most Negro League ballplayers, we often had to play more than one position. That was virtually unheard of in the Majors! Pitchers would play the outfield and the infield. Every catcher would double as a first or second baseman. I myself sometimes played third base or outfield while our other catcher, Bill Cash, caught, or vice-versa. And we had to be ready at any time to fill in for up to a week.

But because a guy *could* do more than one thing, that's how we got by if someone got injured or sick. (Though you'd best get well soon, because somebody else could easily take your job away!) And the more positions you could play, the higher your odds for getting hired in the first place.

Bill "Ready" Cash

Again, there was no special training involved for this except staying in shape and on your toes. Unless you were a utility player, you simply focused on practicing your regular position every day, and made the adjustment when you had to. Such flexibility actually gave us a certain advantage over white teams, and kept things interesting for us players.

Because we played all over the country, you had to learn to be able to play in all different kinds of ball fields—including some that were quite rustic. Baseball, in general, is a game where things change every day. For instance, the type of game you play will depend on not only who you're playing but where. Well, we played on different kinds of turf and in different climates. And when you're in the big cities playing in Major League ballparks, you of course play by the rules of that park.

For example, in all Major League parks, if balls were hit fair and they bounced over the fence, that'd be an automatic two-base hit. Foul balls were always in play. And of course the fans always complicated matters by reaching over the fence to bother players trying to catch the balls.

Also, different stadiums had different dimensions. And there was usually a yellow line around the outfield so that the umpires could make a decision on whether the ball went into the stands or whether it hit the wall, and so forth. The placement of that line varied according to which stadium you were playing. So we learned that it's good to scope out a field before you played there, although over time we played in the same places so often we got to know the peculiarities of each one. In smaller towns, we'd often have no idea what their field would be like, but we didn't care. We could wing it.

We had two home fields. One was at Shibe Park, 21st and Lehigh Avenues in northeast Philadelphia (which has long since been torn down and redeveloped). The other was at 44th and Parkside avenues in southwest Philly. Citizens Bank Park, the state-of-the-art stadium where the Phillies now play, wasn't even imagined yet.

Shibe was where the Phillies and Athletics played, and it was among the best ballparks in the Major Leagues: big, beautiful, and well maintained. Monday was always a traveling day for the Major League teams of Philadelphia, so that's when we got to use it. I used to love to hit home runs there.

But I used to hate to come to the ballpark at 44th and Parkside. It was filthy. Coal-powered trains used to pull in nearby at Belmont and Girard avenues for cleaning, then roll back downtown to the main station at 30th Street. Smoke and soot used to waft right into the ballpark. Why, if you went outside with a white shirt on, 20 minutes later that shirt would turn black! Sometimes we even had to stop the games until the smoke blew away.

We always got a great audience in both places. When the Phillies or Athletics would play a double header on Sunday in Shibe Park, capacity 30-plus thousand, they'd draw ten or twelve thousand people. On the following Monday night, the Philadelphia Stars would play a twilight double-header and completely fill the stands!

And not just with black fans. There was an enormous white audience for black baseball, almost 50-50 in Philadelphia. In fact, sometimes we'd play at the park at 44th and Parkside, and get more white patrons than black. They were locals who simply loved baseball, and we were *just that good.*

On the diamond, opposing Negro League teams were enemies and fierce competitors. We'd knock each others' brains out and there was nothing we would not do to win.

Whenever the remaining Philadelphia Stars get together, and that's often, we compare notes on what we were like when we were playing—such as what we planned to do when certain hitters were up to bat and runners were in certain positions. The infielders were going to make the almost impossible play, the pitcher was going to make the good pitch, and the catcher was going to get any changes the hitter made if any to compensate.

For example, we had certain hitters that would swing at breaking balls only for three innings. After six innings it would change. The steal of a base, a bunt with two outs, and a runner on third would cross up anyone. It was common for a base runner to go from first to third on a bunt fielded by the third baseman. We scored runs without those hits. We also had base runners who would steal home by sliding through the hitter's legs.

Another pet play was to pick runners off third base, especially with right-handed hitters at bat. The pitcher would knock the hitter down, giving a clear shot at third base. The runner was usually busy watching the hitter duck the pitch, so he'd be an easy out with a good throw.

Of course, such moves take guts and skill to do, and plays like that happen only two or three times a year, usually in a really big competition like a playoff or World Series, where a game is on the line. Big plays in big games, that's how we played.

The wild, crazy things the Stars and all of the Negro Leagues teams did, angered some. They were just a laugh for us. In fact, it ticks me off when people call ballplayers who play with flair and style "hot dogs." If they have played that way from the time they were three years old, they aren't showboating, that's how they play, and what's wrong with being entertaining? Negro League players like Willie Mays and Oscar Charleston may have looked like they were performing, but only because they got to balls that Babe Ruth, Joe DiMaggio, and Ty Cobb had no chance to get to and couldn't hope to make.

Yet we were good sports, too: There was no such thing as charging the mound when the ball came close to hitting you. There were ways to play so that every player knew that retaliation was in order if he insisted on being stupid. There was a joy to outdo your opponent today, for tomorrow he would outdo you. I have never believed that winning was the only thing—but it's probably the next best thing!

The Stars usually did win our home games—even if we were playing one of the top teams, like the Homestead Grays. And afterwards, enemies became buddies. We ate together and talked about our families and were genuinely nice to each other. I daresay we considered ourselves gentlemen and tried to be worthy of the title. Of course, there were some no one wanted to be close to, and they were lonely unless they changed. My rule was not to bother with anyone unpleasant, so I couldn't even tell you their names.

We sure had a lot of fun before games and after hours, because Philadelphia was hopping. Movies were a great escape: You could go watch from 11 o'clock in the morning until 11 o'clock at night for about 50 cents. One place in particular on 11th and Market streets also offered live musical performances in addition to the films, so you could see the big bands, like Duke Ellington's and Count Basie's, when they were in town.

At night, the players frequented Philadelphia's lively clubs and cheap restaurants. In the '40s, the city had many small jazz and other music venues, which attracted black and white audiences alike. We always used to go hear jazz at the Blue Notes on Ridge Avenue, or big-band music at a particular hotel at Broad and Lombard streets.

Also, there were so many honky-tonk bars and nightclubs along South Street, all of which had top entertainment. South Street was then a Jewish and black ghetto where you could find all sorts of good food. That came in handy, because when I started out, our meal money was only $2 a day. Everything was near the center of town, so transportation was good.

We also patronized the service businesses run by African Americans or those that were willing to serve us. For example, for about $40 I used to get all my suits made to measure at Creation Tailors, a haberdashery at Broad and South streets. Athletes from other Negro League teams who were in town to play the Stars used to flock there, because they knew that they could stop by at 9 a.m. and by the time the ballgame was over, their new suits would be ready! That was an improvement on places like Washington, D.C. Most of those stores wouldn't let you try things on before you bought them.

Fun on and off the field in one of America's sports capitals—it didn't get much better than that.

Barnstorming

Home games—being home in Philly, period—were the exception and not the rule. The Philadelphia Stars were constantly on the road. Like the rest of the Negro League teams, we spent about half of our time playing in the fine Major League ballparks and the rest barnstorming all over the country. That meant touring all over making brief stops along the way.

Oh, now and then we might stay in town for a couple of weeks so we could play some of the Industrial League teams and others within about 150 miles of the city—Stroudsburg and Soderton and Doylestown and every place in between. Then again, most of today's major highways hadn't been built yet, so even driving to someplace relatively close was a trek. Traveling to Warminster, PA, up Route 611, was a big deal because it could take two hours to go 20 miles!

Granted, the Stars probably traveled fewer miles than the other teams because there were so many

NEW YORK BLACK YANKEES

The **New York Black Yankees** were the doormats of the league during my time—they weren't a great team, but had some good players, and their home field was Yankee Stadium!

Zack Clayton, a great former basketball player from Philadelphia, played first base and had some power. **Hack Barker** was a center fielder who was a good hitter and also served as manager. Jim Williams was the left fielder; he could really hit. **John Hardy** was a shortstop with range, and Johnny Hayes was a solid catcher. **Thad Christopher** was a catcher, outfielder, and infielder with fair power.

The strongest part of their team was the pitching staff. **Nick Stanley** was their best, spitball and all, a left-handed pitcher who was sensational. He and Hack Barker were All Stars, great players on an otherwise mediocre team. **Bob Griffith** was a really good pitcher, except that he tipped off his pitches. Still, he had good control and a real live fastball. **Connie Rector** had a great assortment of breaking balls that kept hitters off balance.

The Black Yankees had originated in Harlem, and were once owned by the legendary dancer **Bill "Bojangles" Robinson**, then by a financier and numbers runner named **James "'Soldier Boy"' Semler**.

major stadiums up and down the East Coast—New York, Newark, Baltimore, Washington, and Pittsburgh—and we played in all of them. But at other times we might have to travel over a thousand miles to our destination.

But unlike the Major League teams, who rode in trains and planes to get to other cities, Negro League teams couldn't afford the tickets. Plus, segregation made it difficult for a couple dozen black men to travel together like that. So we had to go by team bus.

I'll tell you, that made for some long trips. Why, if we were going from Philadelphia to some place like Kansas City for a game, we could count on looking out the window of that bus for about three days.

The back-and-forth could be nuts. Say we took a trip to Chicago, which is something like 800 miles from Philadelphia. That might take you 18 hours to drive now, but back then, we didn't have the Pennsylvania Turnpike running across the state. So it was a difficult journey.

Worse, it wasn't uncommon for us to play a double-header in Chicago on a Sunday, leave at around 6 p.m., then drive all the way back to Philadelphia, because we'd have another double-header waiting for us over at Shibe Park on Monday night. We'd typically arrive home at 4 p.m. and pretty much jump off the bus and start playing.

(You might imagine after all that traveling we'd be half-asleep at bat, but we were always wide awake. We had to be. Besides, it felt good to be back on our own turf.)

Other teams had it as bad or worse. Since they had such a long way to travel between stations, if there was a Negro World Series between, say, Birmingham and Newark, the competition might take four weeks to finish!

(On top of that, at the end of the season, we'd sometimes go out to the West Coast for some games with Major League All Star teams. But when their teams started to expand out to the coast in the mid-1950s, the commissioner declared that at least two or three teams had to be willing to relocate out there if they were going to play one another. For East Coast teams, 3,000 miles for one ballgame was just too far to travel.)

Whatever the destination, we'd begin our journeys the same way, hanging out in front of the YMCA building at 17th and Christian streets in South Philly. If we were going out to the Midwest, we'd hit the road at 6 o'clock in the morning. Our manager, Oscar Charleston, was sure to let everyone know the time the bus was leaving, and it split on the dot. If you were not there, you were left behind. It made no difference who you were, and if you hadn't gotten permission to be late beforehand, it was your tough luck. You simply caught up to the team the best way you could.

The ride ahead could be boring, and gritty, and tiring. See, these weren't rock-star vehicles with TVs, bars, and groupies but simple workhorses on wheels that resembled a Greyhound or a school bus. It wasn't swank, but it was livable. The seats went back a little bit, but there was no way you could ever get comfortable. If it was hot, we opened a window—no vehicles had air-conditioning back then. And if you wanted to wash and shave, you'd pull into a service station and use the little sink in the restroom. We had a driver, but sometimes on long trips one of us players would spell him and take over a while at the wheel.

Often enough, we'd eat on the bus, change clothes on the bus, and sleep on the bus. We didn't have too many other choices. Segregation, discrimination, and inhumanity were just the way America was, and you simply had to accept it.

For example, in or near a city, there might be some kind of fleabag hotel we could stay at, but not so in the country. Mom-and-pop motels and inns would flat-out refuse us. Getting ourselves fed could be difficult, too. Of course, when our teams were at home, we tended to eat well because our wives or mothers cooked for us. But on the road in unfamiliar places, we'd eat what we could get when we could get it.

Back then, there were no Howard Johnson or other type of restaurants that cater to travelers as they do today. Fast-food chains like Wendy's and McDonald's didn't exist yet, so you couldn't just pull in and grab a burger from a drive-through window. (Maybe that's a good thing, because we would have gotten fat and out-of-shape quickly.)

Where there were black-owned businesses like diners around, we'd patronize them. Some places refused to serve blacks altogether, so often enough we'd just have to buy takeout. But there was no way you could even dream about strolling into a café or grocery store and say "I want so and so," get it, and walk away. And the ones who would serve you made you go around to the back door, where they might sell you the ingredients to slap together a sandwich, and a quart bottle of Nehi soda.

Traveling between cities and barnstorming in those small towns along the highways and byways, we were often denied meals, fuel, or air for our tires. Some gas stations would flat-out refuse to fill our bus. Sometimes we could get around that by being resourceful—we'd start filling up the tank, then the people at the snack bar next door would tell us they didn't serve black folk. (Only they weren't that polite.) So we'd say, "Take that gas hose out of my truck. I'm not gonna buy any gas if I can't buy any food." And they'd relent—few in America would turn down a dollar for a principle!

Other times, we could not get fuel and the bus would break down. So we'd wait until we saw somebody walking along the highway and they might tell you about a farmer or a place down the road that had some gas. They'd sell us some so we could move on—they didn't want us there in the first place! Because of that, we rarely waited till we were flat out to pull up to a pump.

That sort of thing didn't just happen in Georgia and Kentucky, but all over. We often endured the same treatment in northern states, especially in suburbs and rural areas. Even in my state of Pennsylvania, between Philadelphia and Harrisburg and between Harrisburg and Pittsburgh, most hotels and restaurants were off-limits to us.

As you might expect, we did have a large share of trouble down in the Bible Belt region. By the way, I don't know why they call it that, because there was nothing holy about it! Separation of the races was law and custom, with signs saying "Whites Only," and you'd better not challenge it.

Travel back with me a moment to Memphis, Tennessee, where the Stars were going to stay for a few days. We played three games in the city—one on Saturday and two on Sunday. Then, on the weekdays, we'd go over to play in nearby towns, and finally go back to Memphis that evening because unlike the small burgs, they had hotels where they'd let us stay.

One time in about 1948, as the team bus first pulled in to the town of Clarksville, Mississippi, the police flagged us down. A cop climbed in and insulted us using the N-word. Then he told us, "The home game tonight

---

THE MEMPHIS RED SOX

I got to be real close with some of the ballplayers of the **Memphis Red Sox**. They had a left-handed pitcher, **Verdell Mathis**, who was really, really great. I used to call him Cousin. He could throw with both hands if he wanted to, it wouldn't make any difference. I used to hit home runs off of him—he couldn't get me out. Yes, I had some great days in Memphis. Lots of home runs and a real good hitting ballpark.

One who's still alive now is **Joe B. Scott**, a fine infielder. Then there was **Wesley "Doc" Dennis**, a good hitter and a fine fielder who eventually joined the Stars as a first baseman.

Several from Memphis went to the Majors: pitchers **Dan Bankhead** (hired by the Dodgers not long after Jackie Robinson); another pitcher, **Jehosie Heard**, who became the first black player in the Baltimore Orioles; and first baseman **Bob Boyd**, first black player in the Chicago White Sox.

Dr. J.B. Martin was the team's owner. Martin was a dentist, and you didn't find many black dentists at that time. But he was successful enough that he built a ballpark for the Red Sox to play in, in Memphis. He was quite a guy—never heard anything negative about him.

will be over by 10 o'clock or I'm gonna lock up all of you ballplayers, and then it will be over! Thanks very much." When we asked why, the officer told us that only white men and black women were allowed on the streets after that hour. That meant we had to ride more than 100 miles in sweaty, dirty uniforms back to where we were staying in Memphis.

Things like that happened all over the South when we were playing, because of curfews. They didn't allow black men and white women on the street alone past 10 o' clock. In fact, it was routine to be stopped by the police for no reason at all. They would then use racial slurs and laugh about it before letting us go on our way.

What we experienced wasn't just rude and inconvenient. It could be downright dangerous. I'm sure you've heard about the lynching and other senseless murders of blacks by whites on the flimsiest excuse. Nothing like that ever happened to us Negro League players, because we knew better. A good number of players were from the deep South, and if we didn't know they'd tell us how it was. You had to know how to act in order to stay safe: Always travel in a group. Mind your manners and don't insult anybody. And be very, very careful about looking anyone in the eye. You did what you were supposed to do, and that was it. And if you didn't know what you were supposed to do, they put you in jail.

Like I said, there was nothing holy about that Bible Belt. Which is a shame because I'm *from* the South and it has many wonders. One time, I remember sitting in the bus driving back through Meridien, Mississippi. Meridien is probably the prettiest place I've ever been in my life. The trees beside the highway make a natural arch over the road, so it's cool there even when it's 99 degrees outside. I asked myself, How can these people be so mean with all of this beauty?

We endured the insults and indignities because when we piled off that bus, we got to do our favorite thing: play baseball.

Barnstorming through America was a heck of a lot of fun. We played in the many small towns in Pennsylvania, New York, New Jersey, Delaware, Maryland, and Virginia. We played deep in the heartland of Kansas and Nebraska, in hamlets and farm communities where

---

BARNSTORMING

When many people hear the word "**barnstorming**," they think about stunt-flying and airplane exhibitions in the 1920s. The term originally referred to pilots selling airplane rides to folks in small towns, where they used farmers' fields as runways. Soon enough, it came to mean simply touring from place to place in rural areas while making brief stops. Barnstormers included theater troupes, politicians, and of course, baseball teams.

people had to stand to watch. We played in places where people would come up on horseback and stay in the saddle for the entire game. Not only that, we played just about every day. That made record-keeping difficult, since many places were so small or remote they didn't have a daily paper.

We took on any team who had a good following and thought they could beat us. Often that would be a local league, black or white. When we arrived, people would greet us and brag that their local boys were going to win. Of course, they ended up losing miserably. It didn't register that we were professionals. They only knew we were black and assumed we were on their level!

Playing such small-town teams, who were basically amateurs, was a pleasure. We always whipped them! But we didn't go in there with the intention of shaming them. We wanted a good game—we'd just make sure that in the end, we'd win.

We loved those games because the businesses and manufacturers of those towns would promote their teams with great fanfare. I don't know what they got out of it, except community pride. Everybody who lived in these little towns would always come out to stand around or sit in a lawn chair or the stands and watch the games. It was jolly, and gave people a place to go for entertainment that was affordable and close by.

I saw how good it was for the neighborhoods. It gave the children something to do instead of running around in the street doing who-knows-what, because they had baseball. And once people figured out it didn't cost a fortune to put lights up at local ballparks, most of them did. Of course, it was pretty basic and not very bright, but you could see well enough to play. Today's suburbs and cities have built modern baseball facilities for residents, but you seldom see people out playing. It's a shame.

In these small towns, it was hard to find lodging before or after the competition. Fortunately, we were able to depend on the kindness of strangers along the way. We'd stay in the private homes of baseball fans who were gracious enough to host us overnight.

See, we were often on the road on weekends, and on Sunday you'd go to the local church the same as you would have if you'd been at home. Wherever we were, we'd always find black folks at church, so you'd meet the people of the congregation and introduce yourself to the pastor. You could ask around about who might have an extra room with a bed or a couch to put up two guys here or three guys there, and make arrangements.

So we'd stay there, and they'd cook dinner and breakfast for us, and we'd eat at the table and have wonderful conversations with their families. Everyone would share stories about our games and where we'd been and something about our backgrounds, and they'd tell us about their communities, their friends, and their activities.

Because of this, we got acquainted with all sorts of people from every region of this country, up close and personal. I made some long-term friendships that way, especially in the South. Sadly, all of these fine people have long since passed.

We also had many generous fans in the big cities. People were willing to pay the same money to see Negro League games as they did to watch the big-name teams. In Yankee Stadium, we played to crowds of 30,000 and 40,000, and in the Polo Grounds, 20,000 to 30,000. In Newark's Ruppert Stadium and Baltimore's Bugle Field, we would fill the park, and people would stand up to watch the games. In fact, it wasn't uncommon for attendance at Negro League games to exceed it at Major League events.

And though our teams were segregated by race, the stands in the stadiums were integrated with fans of all colors who just wanted to watch a great game—at least in places like Chicago, Indianapolis, Kansas City, and Detroit. Not so in the South though. In places like Memphis and Birmingham, you might see a sprinkling of diehard white folk, but most of the spectators were black.

After those games, the fans honored us—and the appreciation was mutual. We enjoyed signing autographs, and we never said no or charged. We aimed to please all who came to the ballpark, and we did it with grace. During my seven-year career, probably 100 people invited me to dinner, especially on Sundays.

We were also often welcomed to the houses of the elite to make merry. Our hosts included prominent families such as the Spaldings of Chicago, who were big in politics at that time, and the Yancys of Philadelphia. Bill Yancy was a former Stars player who owned a popular restaurant on Broad and South streets after he retired. Those parties after games were unforgettable, with fantastic food, flowing beverages, and music, music, music.

In these bustling urban areas, there were more options for us traveling black ballplayers, especially above the Mason-Dixon Line. Once you knew your way around the neighborhoods, you could find plenty of black-run restaurants and businesses where you could dine or shop and enjoy a bit of variety. We never went anyplace really fancy, but you could at least go and get supper and not be harassed or thrown out by bigoted owners or patrons.

And come evening, we were welcomed at all of the culture hubs. We hung out with the patrons at jazz clubs, and you could always find a theater where the big bands and top vocalists were playing to enthusiastic crowds. We'd mingle with the other athletes there, and after we saw the shows we'd go up and introduce ourselves to the musicians and celebrities who were touring those cities at the same time.

For example, bandleader and vibraphone player Lionel Hampton was a huge baseball lover. Singer and movie star Lena Horne was starting to have great success, and often performed in the nightspots of Pittsburgh. Oh, she was gorgeous! Both were loyal fans of Negro League baseball, and as far as they were concerned, we ballplayers were stars in our own right. We'd always hang around and talk with them wherever they were having a show.

THE CHICAGO AMERICAN GIANTS

The **Chicago American Giants** was one of the top-winning teams. One of the memorable names that come to mind here is **Lonnie Summers**, who was a big hitter. He played outfield and could hit the ball really hard. Then there was **Bobby Robinson**, a fine infielder who actually played before my time. He was known as the "Human Vacuum" because he could catch a ball anywhere near him. **Lester Lockett** played several positions for the Giants. Lester hit with power and consistency and was always ready to play. He was on almost all of the Negro League teams at some point!

I also remember a pitcher by the name of **Jeep Jessup**. He was an All Star many years in a row. I didn't care for him personally, though: He was a mean rascal!

Speaking of pitchers, **Double Duty Radcliffe** was with them when I came in the league. Now there was a character—he just passed away in the summer of 2005 at 103 years old. A sportswriter named Damon Runyon nicknamed him "Double Duty" because in the 1932 World Series he caught the first game of a double header and pitched the second. It was a shut-out! Duty alternated pitched and caught his whole career. Besides Chicago, he played for everybody, and he had a brother named **Alex Radcliffe** who was a pretty decent ballplayer too.

This team was created by the one and only **Rube Foster** out of the old Leland Giants. Under his leadership, they won 11 championships. Sometimes he even filled in as their pitcher! After he died, management passed on to another great player, and infielder named **Dave Malarcher**, and later Dr. J.B. Martin.

Pittsburgh in particular was a fun place to be. Gus Greenlee had built a ballfield there and ran two night-clubs, Greenlee I and Greenlee II. He was a close friend of Oscar Charleston, which was how I came to meet him. He also owned the Crawford Grill, which was *the* place to eat and socialize. Gus may have had some shady side businesses, but he was a decent man and never hurt anyone.

We always liked going to Kansas City, too. The ballpark was always full, especially when Satchel Paige was pitching. Kansas City was a mecca for people in the music business and a great place to find entertainment, and still is. All the best clubs were located at Eighteenth and Vine streets. Chicago had its own scene, but I never much cared for the Windy City. I'm not sure why.

Now, in places like Birmingham and Memphis, there were only certain places that black people were allowed to go, so that's where we all assembled. That way, we got acquainted with so many of the black businesspeople and restaurant and club owners in the region.

Unfortunately, there are ignorant people wherever you go, and we still had racist incidents in cities, I don't care if it was Atlanta or Brooklyn.

Some were pretty minor, and you could slough it off. One time, the Philadelphia Stars were staying in Birmingham, Alabama, while we traveled to surrounding towns during the week to play the Black Barons. As games go sometimes, the score was up and down. We would score four runs, and then the Barons would come back and score five runs. We were sitting in the bullpen at one point and a white fellow came down to talk to us. The man was so drunk he could barely walk. Very politely he said, "I bet money you northern niggers were going to beat the southern niggers. Now you better not let them niggers catch up again, you hear?" After one more chug from the moonshine he was carrying, he fell asleep.

We'd heard that word more times than anyone could count. I don't believe that guy was a bad person. No doubt that was the way his parents talked, so they probably taught him to talk that way, too. He'd basically lived in a matchbox all his life and probably died never leaving that matchbox.

Other incidents were outrageous. One in particular stands out in my mind. One night, the Stars were out in Indianapolis, Indiana for a game. Now, Indianapolis is a big, Midwestern city that happened to be Oscar Charleston's hometown. We went into a hotel restaurant and were waiting to place our order when a policeman strode in and wanted to know what we were doing there.

"Well," we said, "We're a baseball team, and we're here for the night and waiting for dinner." He didn't like that, and for no reason at all locked up the entire ballclub in jail. He didn't even bother to tell us why or trump up some charges like disorderly conduct. He did it because he could.

THE BIRMINGHAM BLACK BARONS

The **Birmingham Black Barons** were another one of the most successful teams. For starters, they're the team that **Howard "Willie" Mays**, one of the greatest who ever played, started with at the tender age of 16.

Mays played center field. He was just a kid, with a squeaky little voice, young and crazy and about nine-and-a-half cents short of a dime! We all liked being around him, because he had a great sense of humor and was a playful person. On the field, there wasn't anything he couldn't do, and he did it better than anybody else. And he did more things very, very *well* than anybody else.

What's more, I don't know anyone with more baseball savvy than Mays. Most players have to put in their mind on the game—"What am I going to do if the ball is hit to me?" and so on. Well, Mays didn't have to think about it, he just did it. It was that instinctive. He always seemed to know when the ball was going to be hit, he always caught it, and he was the one who used to catch triples. That's more than I can say about 95 percent of ballplayers. No matter how good they are, there has to be some soul-searching when it comes down to making plays, or running when you should run. Mays ran when he should *not* have run and still made it!

Once he got into the majors, starting with the Giants, he could run, throw, steal bases, hit for average, and hit home runs, right up there with Babe Ruth and Hank Aaron. There were many who thought Mays was in a class by himself. If they could have made a league higher than the majors, Willie would have led that league.

Another important player was shortstop **Artie Wilson**, who very briefly went into the Major Leagues.

The Barons' manager was one **Lorenzo "Piper" Davis**, the guy who signed Mays. He was also quite a player—started out at second base and went to first base in his later years, and got a tryout with the Boston Red Sox organization when he was way past his prime—the first black player they took.

Well, when you're arrested everybody gets one phone call. I was acting secretary of the Stars and my call was to Eddie Gottlieb, who ran the ballclub. Eddie started cursing.

"Where are you?!" he asked.

"I'm in jail in the station house in Indianapolis!" I replied.

"Tell somebody to pick up the phone," Eddie demanded. And when he got finished with those people they found a bus, put us on it and sent us back to our hotel.

I later asked him, "How much money did you have to pay them to fix it?"

Eddie scoffed. "I wouldn't give them a dime! I chewed 'em out. Told 'em you'd better let my ballclub out, or I'll come down and Indiana won't be there when I leave!"

That was the traveling, barnstorming life for you: It could bring elation or anguish at any time—sometimes both in the same day.

From My Perspective

Making baseball my vocation was turning out to be an absolute ball. By now I'd had a couple years' experience under my belt, although it was interrupted for a while because I had to go serve in World War II. I was on par with my teammates and could appreciate the fine points of Negro League baseball from the inside—crouched behind the plate in my catcher's pose.

BLACK BALL DURING WARTIME

My baseball career was interrupted in September 1945, when I was drafted into the U.S. Army. They had to do that, because I never would have signed up on my own!

I wound up serving as an operating-room technician in the Army Medical Corps. They sent me to Denver, Colorado, for training in the best general hospital in the city. I liked the work, but the following spring, I started pulling whatever strings I could to get as close as possible to the East Coast.

Well, I wound up serving at Camp Adderbury near Lafayette, Indiana. My job was working on a hospital ship, bringing home men who'd gotten shot up and injured on the front lines. Sometimes we'd be out two or three months at a time, and I missed most of the '46 baseball season.

But like many Negro League players who were called to duty during World War II, nothing could stop me from playing for long, and I rejoined the game whenever I could get leave. Every now and then I'd work so many days straight, then take five or six days off. I'd get a train or an overnight flight and come to Philadelphia and they'd put me in.

My teammate Mahlon Duckett had that arrangement for almost his entire Army career. He managed to play Baltimore and Washington, Philadelphia and Newark—anywhere there was a train every hour on the hour. Our military commanders didn't care where you went in your spare time—as long as you were there for reveille in the morning.

I was finally discharged in November of 1946, and between baseball seasons took some additional training in physical therapy at the Philadelphia School of Physical Medicine. I never did use it—the closest job available in the field at that time was in Guam, and the salary was $3,600 a year. Decent pay, but I stuck with baseball. Only now I had new nickname: Doc!

Naturally, what I remember of the games and the players is from that perspective. But that's fine, because baseball, at heart, is a game of cat and mouse between the pitcher and catcher against the hitter. In fact, the Stars won most of our games from pitching and defense.

Let me explain my stance. When you're the catcher, you have to manipulate. And you have to know the desires of your pitcher and the nature of the team you're playing against. No matter who the opposition is, hitters are looking for certain pitches depending on what the count is on the pitcher. So you have to keep the hitter at bay by doing the opposite of what he's looking for so that he does not get the fat of the bat on the ball.

In other words, you have to do the unexpected in terms of the kinds of pitches you call. And I happened to be one of those catchers that lived and died on the unexpected.

My strategy behind the plate was to signal my pitcher that he had six targets to throw at. Besides the catcher's glove, there are the two knees, the two shoulders, and the head. A smart hitter will always be looking out of the corner of his eye at the catcher's position so he gets an idea of what kind of pitch is coming. But just because the glove is in a certain place doesn't mean that that's the target the pitcher intends to hit! And while the hitter can see the glove out of the corner of his eye, it's very difficult for him to see the rest of you.

SNEAKY PITCHES

Certain types of sneaky pitches involved changing the physics of the baseball itself, to throw the hitter off. For instance, with a **spitball**, the pitcher would dab saliva on the ball. For a **greaseball**, he'd put hair tonic on it. A **cut ball** had been cut into it with a nail or a belt buckle to make the ball jump. And for an **emery ball**, the pitcher would rub the ball with sandpaper, which would make it do crazy things! A **screwball** was a pitch that curves to the same side it was thrown from. In a **forkball**, the pitcher would clutch the ball with two fingers, which tended to make it head downwards. And a **junk baller** was a pitcher who used a variety of pitches at different speeds.

Bill Cash, the other catcher in my time, had his own style. Naturally I believe I was the better of the two players. Bill was older than me and came in a year before, but no matter what anyone says, he never coached me. My "six-point strategy" was my own invention. Even so, we always traded tips and ideas. We were on the same team, so we had the same goals.

I also worked pitchers differently than most other catchers—I simply believed that all hitters are my meat if my pitcher can throw strikes with three or four different pitches. The way I see it, a good catcher makes ordinary pitchers good, good pitchers better, and all pitchers *think*.

Most great pitchers have a good fastball, a good curve ball and a change-up, and they often change speeds on all their pitches, with the ability to throw all of the pitches for strikes. Trick pitches, like screwballs, forkballs, split fingers and any others that are thrown with unnatural throws and releases, are real arm-breakers.

So, when a pitcher can throw strikes with several different pitches, and the catcher calls all those pitches, even the best hitters will be moaning and groaning. The Philadelphia Stars had many fastball pitches, and I got more outs from their specialty pitches than I did from the bread-and-butter ones.

Also, whereas most other catchers would refuse to call the pitch a hitter hits best, I'd go ahead and signal the pitcher to throw any hitter any pitch at any time in the right location and I'd get him out most of the time. My pitchers believed in me and trusted my judgment, and we had great fun.

Many catchers, too, refuse to call certain pitches with runners on base, because their weaknesses would show. Some could not throw well after receiving breaking pitches; others had trouble catching balls that were in the dirt, high or wide.

But the truth is, you have to be able to fake out the hitter in order to get the pitcher through when he doesn't have his best stuff that particular day. And all pitchers have off days.

Wilmer Harris

I noticed most of our pitchers had pet mannerisms that appeared when they were in trouble. After a base hit, Joe Filmore threw the next pitch harder than the last, but usually not for a strike, because he was overthrowing. Bob Griffith always stuck his tongue out when he was throwing his curve ball. Wilmer Harris sometimes would tip his curve ball by gripping it differently. Now because he was one of my pitchers, I told him to grip it in the familiar way—and then throw a fastball.

Sometimes a pitcher's best pitch won't get anyone out, so the element of surprise was his best pitch that day. For instance, one night, the Stars were playing a team in Ontario, Canada, and Wilmer Fields was pitching. I never saw so many line drives hit in my life! He couldn't get anybody out.

Later he confided, "You haven't said a word. Do you know what's wrong?"

I said, "Sure. You've got it in your mind that you can throw your curveball anytime you want and you're gonna get 'em out. Now, you know you can't. What I think you should do is take about half off how hard you're throwing the ball, for both the fast ball and curve ball." That way, he could mess with the hitters' timing. Sure enough, it did the trick.

THE KANSAS CITY MONARCHS

The Kansas City Monarchs was a real winning team—they won the NAL pennant seven times—and two of the leagues' most famous players were on the team during my own career: **Jackie Robinson**, of course, and pitcher Satchel Paige. They were always near the top and a tough team to beat. But we sometimes did beat them—they couldn't come to Philadelphia and take out anything!

Even after all these years I can tell you just about everybody that was on that team. **John "Buck" O'Neil**, who now heads the Negro League Baseball Museum, was the first baseman, and later their manager. **Barney Surrell** was the second baseman, **Herb Sewell** was on third, and the shortstop was **Jesse Williams.** All of them were All Stars.

They had a fellow who played the outfield, **Willard Brown**, who was quite a guy—he made the St. Louis Browns when he was close to 40 years old, and was one of the first after Jackie to go to the majors. The Monarchs also had a catcher by the name of **Ike Brown** (no relation), who was excellent—a home run hitter who went to the majors.

You may remember Jackie Robinson as a first baseman, but in the Negro Leagues he was the Monarch's shortstop. He only played a little less than one season before the Dodgers took him.

Of course, Robinson would have been a blue-chip player in any league, not because his baseball skills were superior (though they sure weren't cream cheese). No, it was but because he had the heart, the soul, and the will to do whatever it took to succeed.

Of course there was great **Satchel Paige**, pitcher par excellence. He'd played with any number of Negro League teams since the '20s, but was with the Monarchs when I played. He threw a funny fastball called the "bee ball" that made the ball seem small. Satchel had pinpoint control, and catching him was actually easy.

This was a man with confidence: he'd call the outfielders in, then proceeded to strike out three straight. Once he joined the majors—and he was an old man in his 40s at the time—this same Satchel would tell Joe DiMaggio to get ready to hit his fastball, because that was all he was going to throw him. Although he knew what was coming, DiMaggio might've got four hits off him in about 50 times at bat. If the ghost of Joe is looking down, I'd tell him not to feel too bad: Satchel did the same thing to Josh Gibson. He did not believe anyone could hit his fastball, and talked to the hitters like that all the time. I think it was Satchel who coined the saying, "Never look back, someone might be catching up to you." He meant it, too.

As great as Satchel Paige was, there was another pitcher on the Monarchs who was almost as great, **Hilton Smith**. He was the best breaking-ball pitcher I've ever seen. He never hung a curve ball that I can remember, and was a real artist on the mound.

If you did not get any runs off of Satchel, you'd already lost, because Hilton followed Satchel and you were not getting any off of him, either. Sometimes these days I forget his name, but I wouldn't want to remember much because he used to get me out pretty easily!

J.L. Wilkinson, the white former ballplayer who started the NAL, was the Monarchs' owner. Wilkinson came up with the idea of night baseball years before the Major Leagues—by rigging up a portable lighting system at games. **Tom Baird**, a quiet, immaculate businessman, was a co-owner during the time I played. Both of them were real gentlemen.

Wilmer and my other teammates would probably have described me as hard-nosed. Sometimes a catcher just has to go and ream that pitcher out because he's not doing the things he knows darn well he should be. (When the game was over you could go back to being buddies.) Others guys would give you everything you wanted every time you saw them. And at the end of the day over dinner or drinks, my teammates would ask me why I called a particular pitch. My answer would always be, "It worked."

For me, making these judgment calls was all about observation. When playing league ball, you get to know players very well, because there are few changes from year to year. You notice their strengths and weaknesses both as players and as people. As catcher, I learned these tics, because I was positioned so close to them.

For instance, some hitters cursed themselves, some complained to themselves, and some literally cried, but not out of weakness. However, they might hit the very next pitch nine miles. I knew some who stayed loose by humming or talking, and yet they were ready to uncoil. I knew some who were at their best laughing and kidding, and have seen some that concentrated so hard that when the time came they could not execute. Some players were plain nuts—funny, but nine-and-a-half cents short of a dime.

Now, Josh Gibson of the Homestead Grays wasn't human. With my own eyes, I'd watch him hit balls right out of the park. One time was at Griffith Stadium, which measured 405 feet down the left field to the stands, where they had a 20-foot high fence and maybe 20 rows of seats in the left-field bleacher section. Just outside the park were trees where kids would sit to watch the game for free. And Josh would knock those kids right out of the trees!

I also noticed that some hitters seemed to have made a promise with themselves that a pitcher would not get a certain pitch by them. Usually it was a pitch they had trouble handling, so they went up to hit that pitch only. They got mixed results, because most pitchers will throw their best one sooner or later in the count. Seldom did good hitters miss their pitch in a certain area.

I remember one night in Washington, D.C., when the Philadelphia Stars were playing the Kansas City Monarchs, and it was raining cats and dogs. Kansas City was way behind us with almost no chance to win. Jackie Robinson was new to pro ball then and he knew he was going to be the last out that night. He was telling me to get the pitcher to throw him curve balls. He was not a good curve-ball hitter then, but he was gradually improving. That time, he popped up.

The hitters I disliked most were the free swingers, the ones who swung at bad pitches. There wasn't much point in that. Sometimes it could even be funny. During one game against the New York Cubans, their left-handed pitcher, Luis Tiant, Sr., took all his strength and threw the ball to first base—there was a runner on first and he wanted to make sure he stayed there. Meanwhile, our Goose Curry was up at bat. Goose was a simple guy, spacey and plain nuts. So when he saw that move he swung at thin air, as if Tiant had been pitching to *him*! The umpire, Fred McCreary, said, "Goose, I should call a strike!"

You might be surprised to learn that some of the most challenging matches weren't always against the best hitters. It was the guy who hit .250, maybe one hit out of every four times at bat, who'd hurt us most when a game was close. He'd be at his best when the count was down. Most of the time, those guys turned out to be the most valuable players. Games against fellows like that were real nail-biters.

Generalizations like I've just described applied to many games. But it's another story when people ask me to name the most memorable matches, or my all-time favorites. Shoot, if you play something like 2,000 baseball games, it's awfully hard to pick one or two that were the most exciting.

Really, it was a great game any time we played in one of the Major League ballparks, especially against the teams of the West in a four-team double-header.

One time, in 1949, I hit five home runs when the Stars were playing the New York Black Yankees on Sunday in Yankee Stadium. Bob Griffith was the pitcher.

The year before, in 1948, I played in the East-West game on one of the All-Star teams. I came to bat only once. But when you're playing in Comiskey Park, Chicago, and 50,000 people are out there watching you from all over America, and you're playing against the cream of the crop in the whole league, that's pretty thrilling!

That year, I played with or against Roy Campanella, Monte Irvin, Johnny Davis, Len Pearson, Biz Mackey, Henry Miller, Barney Brown, John "Buck" O'Neil, Jesse Williams, Buck Leonard and others. I'm happy to say the East won.

The All-Star exhibition games between the Major Leagues and the Negro Leagues, which took place at the end of each season, were also a big deal and a lot of fun to follow, even if you weren't playing in them. Those had come about in the early '30s, after Baseball Commissioner Landis had nixed games between intact white teams and black ones. But he let the Major Leagues select an All Star team from among the various National and American League teams so they could compete against an All Star lineup of Negro League players from our various teams. The way he figured it, win or lose, the results wouldn't reflect on any one organization.

Well, in 1946, Cleveland Indians pitcher Bob Feller had his Major League All Stars and the Monarchs' Satchel Paige had his black All Stars, and they'd play each other from New York all the way to California. The white team still didn't beat us! They just felt a little better about losing.

(Today when I speak to students about my experiences in the Negro Leagues, I tell them, "Don't underestimate the person that you're playing against. He might beat you!" Of course, there are those of us who refuse to be beat; and that's not too healthy either. I think it's better to walk around with a little smile on your face and say, "OK, I'll take you the next time.")

Winter Ball

Baseball is a summer sport, but Negro League baseball was a year-round thing. For many, including me, that was a matter of economic necessity. We made a living wage, but people needed income all the time, especially if they had a family to support. So during the off-seasons, most of us players took the opportunity to play winter ball on professional teams in Latin America.

We traveled to many of the same countries where we recruited for the Negro Leagues. For example, I myself played for any number of teams in Maracaibo, Puerto Rico; Cuba; Caracas, Venezuela; and Panama.

Down there, it was warm enough to play ball most of the year, and on top of that you could make triple the salary you were making here. You'd negotiate the deal before you left, then typically sail or fly out around the middle of October and stay till Christmas, or sometimes until spring (depending on the country and the team).

Similar to the U.S. Negro Leagues, these winter teams were made up of players from various Latin nations, Canadians, and black Americans. What's more, they also featured white players from the Major Leagues who'd been sent down for extra practice. Seemed like integration was the rule everywhere *but* the USA!

Working in another country had its ups and downs. One difficulty was the language barrier. Puerto Rico and Cuba were good gigs because the weather was similar to Florida's and you didn't need a passport—and of course, the Cuban players were excellent. (I think the reason is, just as a playing pro sports was one of the decent jobs open to an American black man, Cuban boys grew up seeing their fathers come home with blood running down their hands from cutting sugar cane all day. If you had a choice between going into a field and cutting cane and playing baseball for a living, which would you take?) I also made many friends in Panama, where they spoke both Spanish and English, but Venezuela was tough. It was so far from home, and they didn't much like Americans of any race.

Then again, not everyone could go abroad. The Latin nations only allowed so many Americans on each team, so the guys who didn't play winter ball worked regular jobs to keep a roof over their heads. In my case, I found a position in the winter of 1946 at a wholesale electrical supply store in South Philly through my sister, who worked for the family that owned it. That was how I entered a second profession that would one day provide me with a career lasting some 30 years.

All told, between traveling to local games, barn-storming, and playing winter ball, a Negro League ballplayer might be away most of the year, and only get home five or six days a month. That was a hardship for our loved ones, so we made accommodations on both sides.

For instance, friends and families of the Philadelphia Stars often followed us to away games along the East Coast. The trip from New York to Washington, D.C. is less than 300 miles so many people traveled between cities to watch us play. Round-trip train fare from Philadelphia to New York or Baltimore was less than five dollars, and about ten dollars to and from Washington. Those who had autos filled them up with fans and drove to the games.

Of course, we met ladies on the road. In fact, Negro League Baseball was a real match-making factory. Since all the pretty girls would come to our games, both at home and away, we players had our pick of the finest to be our wives. On longer trips, some of our spouses would travel with us. When I was about 21, I myself got married for the first time, to a gal named Adele. She was a real baseball fan and I took her just about everywhere with me (except on the team bus).

Even playing in South America, it wasn't uncommon to bring your wife and kids if you could afford it. Sometimes the team would pay for it, if they were wealthy enough and wanted you enough.

But just as often, toting your relatives wasn't practical. That's why this book wouldn't be complete without honoring those girls we married. They were such loyal fans and high-quality individuals that they stayed and kept our homes and raised our children by themselves. They did an excellent job of parenting, too.

At least in Philadelphia, players' wives often lived down the street or around the corner from each other, so when their husbands were away they had a mutual-support system to fall back on. Black families were closer then than they are now, because the tragedy of slavery was closer in memory. Everyone stuck together, and caring for our children was a top priority. Those marriages produced future doctors, lawyers, and teachers.

THE BALTIMORE ELITE GIANTS

The **Baltimore Elite Giants** were quite a team.

Johnnie Washington played first base and had no shortcomings there, and was also a decent hitter. **Junior Gilliam** played second base. While Junior came to Baltimore a talented young man, it was Peewee Butts (below) who stayed with him after games and during mornings to teach him how to play. **Felton Snow** was their third baseman and manager.

Maybe the best shortstop after John Henry "Pop" Lloyd was **Pee Wee Butts**. Pee Wee was small in stature, but you name it, he did it effortlessly. He literally made players cry. Balls hit in the hole that you thought were hits, he made into easy outs. He was always there to retrieve balls hit up the middle, he charged slow balls hit to short, and threw the runner out in the same motion. Pee Wee made the second baseman and first baseman better, yet he was so unassuming, you had to play with him (or against him) many times to appreciate him. And once he'd trained **Junior Gilliam**, they became one of the best combinations I have ever seen. They did it with grace, that's how good they were.

In center field, there was **Henry Kimbro**, who was one of the best of many. He was a fine lead pitcher with extra base power and excellent speed, with a good accurate arm and love of the game.

Wild Bill Wright was the right fielder. We called him Wild Bill because he ran like a horse—like the wind. He also threw very well and was a good hitter.

George Scales, known as Tubby, was an infielder who would take two strikes to wait for the pitcher to throw him a curve ball, and would hit the darnedest line drives to right center and left center you have ever seen.

The Elite Giants had a quality pitching stable led by **Bill Byrd**, a spitballer with a very fine fastball and low strikes. **Andy Porter** had a sneaky fast ball, a decent curve ball and change-up, and threw strikes. **Jonas Gaines** was a crafty, left-handed pitcher. **Bob Romby** was another lefty with an assortment of breaking pitches and a sneaky fastball.

Joe Black was a power pitcher with a heart bigger than life. He was a real champion. What's more, Joe was a real compassionate man, a brotherly guy, a giving and warm human being.

The catchers were **Roy Campanella**, from North Philadelphia, and **Robert "Eggie" Clark**. In Roy, you had finesse, power, hitting, and speed. Watching Roy catch, you can see Biz Mackey's teaching and clutch hitting. I played against him all the time, but we were never on the same team.

The **Baltimore Elite Giants** were owned by **Tom Wilson**. He started the team in Nashville, Tennessee, in the 1920s, and eventually became an officer for the Negro National League.

We all made the sacrifices because it was simply how black ballplayers of the day earned our living. And I think we were more dedicated than any Major

League player of the time or since. Ninety-nine percent of the guys played because they loved to play, and it would not have mattered how much money they were making.

There's a big difference between talent and desire, and these men had both. I've known many guys who had natural talent and their desire to play was almost nil. But with us, if your heart wasn't in it, you weren't going to make it, because the living was hard. Traveling, eating, sleeping: Every walk of life that you have to go through was difficult, and often enough, you'd find yourself pulling a 12-hour day.

Most of us were high school and college graduates who might've had other options, and some of our families would have preferred that we didn't play the sport. So those of us who did were truly passionate about it for its own sake. The conditions that we traveled in, ate in, lived in, and the horrible indignities we swallowed, were all because we loved the game. How else could we have survived, playing winter and summer, leaving our wonderful wives and children for weeks or months at a time?

The thing is, the experiences we shared made all the time we put in worth it. Our life on the road provided many lessons to those of us looking to learn something, and many wonderful people to learn it from. Quite a few players in the Negro Leagues couldn't read or write, and the same was true of men in the Major Leagues. Many ballplayers at that time, both black and white, were from the South, where people started working young and therefore got little or no schooling. This was true even for parts of Western Pennsylvania and Ohio. In fact, I'd had a pretty good education myself, but I think I learned more traveling than I did in school! Traveling broadened our horizons and made us more worldly.

Of course, one of the most important things constant travel did was bond the players together, especially on your own team. After all, if you're sitting beside people for hours and days on end, you get to talking, and you get to know them pretty darn well! Like I said, the Stars socialized after all the games, and also with members of the opposing teams. We lived so close together, in fact, it was almost like a fraternity.

Besides all the time we spent together as a team, we had to stick together as men. There was strength in numbers in the face of the bigotry that was part of those times. If you went off alone, something bad could happen—you might be beaten, or hung, or worse.

Frankly, I wouldn't ever want to live that close to anybody again! But I would do it all again because we had a ball. And today, if one of us gets hurt or needs something or has any kind of trouble, you can believe that one or all of us are going to show up on his doorstep and see that he and his family have whatever they need.

Our baseball brotherhood and the support from our families and fans everywhere taught me the most important lessons of all: that life is more important than hate, and that most people are basically good and decent. In the black world in particular, people would help you to do anything that you wanted to do, as long as it was the *right* thing. Knowing that really helped me deal with the hardships, and keeps me going today.

Someone asked me recently if facing years of bigotry ever made me angry or depressed. Sure, sometimes. But I told her you can't let it get to you or it'll just destroy you. *Don't let anyone take your joy away!* I didn't and I won't. If this story has one message, that's it.

Integration Begins

Segregation was the way the country lived for a long time. It was one reason Commissioner Kenesaw Mountain Landis and his pro baseball cronies got away with publicly stating that black players weren't good enough for the majors. I guess they didn't go to the ballpark much, because if they had, they would have been able to see with their own eyes that we were. I would have felt a lot better if they'd just come out and said, "We own baseball and we'll do what we want, and we don't want any black guys playing!"

I can tell you, when desegregation finally came to pro baseball, it was more an economical decision than a principled choice to give black men a fair chance.

During the 1940s, while the Negro Leagues were thriving, the Major Leagues were in decline. Most of the teams, including the Brooklyn Dodgers, were losing money. That's why Philadelphia Athletics manager Connie Mack had to move his team out of Philadelphia—first to Kansas City, then California. They were only drawing half-a-million or so spectators a season and they simply couldn't afford to operate.

The game needed a pick-me-up, and that turned out to be Jackie Robinson of the Kansas City Monarchs. As the world now knows, Brooklyn Dodgers manager Branch Rickey signed Robinson to play for their farm team, the Montreal Royals, in the fall of 1945.

Well, Robinson reported to Montreal for the 1946 season, and in 1947 headed for spring training with the Dodgers. And when he showed up, he brought Negro League Baseball with him.

At the time, most Major League teams had to get a base hit to score one run. Well, Jackie could score a run *without* a base hit. That was standard for most Negro League players. People were impressed, and other players began to pick up his style. In just two months, they stopped playing the same old, dull game that they had been and started playing our way—daring and dynamic. In *two months*, the lies about black players were put to rest.

In the majors, Robinson was a really good, breaking-ball hitter with authority who made National League Rookie of the Year, was named Most Valuable Player two years later, and went on to become the first black player inducted into the Hall of Fame, in 1962.

Jackie made every Dodger better, even with all those ball-busting power hitters. He was their bread and butter day after day, year after year.

It was no coincidence that from Jackie's time on, baseball became more and more popular. Previously, only the Yankees could consistently draw three million spectators a year. Once baseball was integrated, three million became standard. Everyone was going to see baseball again. Robinson probably saved the game!

They certainly took the right guy. He was smart, he was a great athlete, and had more backbone than anyone I've ever met. Once, when he was in the army, Robinson faced a court martial rather than move to the back of a bus (he won the case). Whatever you told him that he couldn't do you'd better look out, because that's what he was going to do!

Branch Rickey was smart enough to know that the first black man to enter the white Major Leagues was going to be harassed by his teammates and the public, and he made Jackie promise he would offer no hostility for his first few years.

But that doesn't mean it was easy. People would be appalled if they knew all the degrading remarks, name-calling, and almost complete rejection Jackie Robinson suffered from his own teammates. Dixie Walker, a right fielder for the Dodgers who used to be called "the People's Choice," and others from the Deep South, were so prejudiced they couldn't stand him and ended up getting themselves traded, or fired.

Worse, Jackie faced death threats, not just to himself but to members of his family. Just for playing with white men on a baseball team! It was a terrible time, having to fight prejudices not only on the field but in everything else he did. In the face of this, he had had to keep his mouth shut, hold in all the stress, and try not to explode. Of course, once he was established, Rickey turned him loose.

Of course, Jackie's success paved the way for the other teams to hire others out of the Negro Leagues. For instance, the Cleveland Indians signed Larry Dobby in 1947. A second baseman for the Newark Eagles, he was made center fielder because they'd just signed the Yankee's second baseman, Joe Gordon, for second. Larry had never played center before in his life.

Let me show you again the effect of Negro League players on mainstream ball. That same year, Cleveland needed a relief pitcher, so they also brought in Satchel Paige, who must've been near 50 then but was still

> ## THE CLEVELAND BUCKEYES
>
> The **Cleveland Buckeyes** were a pretty good baseball team, and near the top of the Western baseball association.
>
> They had ballplayers like **Sam Jethro**, an outfielder who followed not long after Jackie Robinson into the Majors. They called him 'The Jet' because of his speed, and he was a real base-stealer and four-time All Star. **Willie Grace**, a very fine person, now blind, was also an outfielder. Then there was **Al Smith**, a very good left fielder who was young and crazy. He eventually joined the Cleveland Indians and was with them for many years.
>
> One of their more famous players was a great catcher, **Quincy Trouppe**, who started in five All-Star games. He became their manager for a while, and was great at that too. Quincy got a tryout with the Cleveland Indians in the '50s, when he was an old man of 40.
>
> **Ernie Wright,** another former numbers runner who went on to serve as vice president of NAL, was their owner.

going strong. Al Smith, a black guy who'd last played with the Cleveland Buckeyes, came in at left field. Doby quickly mastered center. Before you know it, Cleveland was winning pennants.

Of course, they already had a great pitching staff. They had Bob Feller, Bob Lemon and Early Wynn and Mike Garcia. They had a fine catcher, too, a nice young guy by the name of Jim Hegan who became a co-chair for the Philadelphia Phillies after his playing days were over. I liked Jim—his style and mine behind the plate were almost the same. It goes to show you black players and white players could work great together, if they gave it half a chance.

However, only the Dodgers and the New York Giants seemed to actually welcome black ballplayers. Philly's own Roy Campanella, for example, joined the Dodgers as a catcher in '48 and became the National League MVP three times, and Monte Irvin, who'd played several positions for the Newark Eagles, went to the Giants in '49. There were a couple of years in which the Giants had eight starting black ballplayers! Pretty soon, the best baseball players in the National League were black.

Of course, some coaches or managers refused to accept their originality—the unique style that had made them Negro Leagues stars. But when you try to take away an athlete's naturalness, you take away parts of his game. That may be why many black players have been called hard to get along with. Great managers like Leo Durocher and Tommy Lasorda got the best from their black players because they simply let them play their game. You can't argue with success.

Like Robinson, those who did make it to the majors had it rough. Many guys will tell you that Larry Doby had it worse than Robinson, though I don't see how that could be. I do know he had an awful hard time in Cleveland because at that point, 1948, he was the only black player in the American League, and the rest of the team didn't want him there. Nobody would even play catch with him! He was a quiet fellow who stayed to himself most of the time.

Not only were the teammates hostile, but in the beginning these black players also suffered anonymous death threats. Worse, when teams signed their black ballplayers, they'd send them to the Minor Leagues first, in places such as Florida, Georgia, North Carolina, and Mississippi, where they *knew* that they were going to have a hard time. I think the teams did that so that the black ballplayers would quit. But they didn't. They hung in there, and when they got to the Major Leagues you could see what kind of athletes they were. These individuals had made up their minds that they weren't going to let segregation keep them down for another hundred years!

I saw this sort of thing firsthand with the Philadelphia Phillies. First off, the Phillies didn't even hire their first black ballplayer until the '50s. They could've had their pick of some very fine players right in the area, but weren't interested. By '55 the Athletics had already left town, so they weren't hiring either.

And when Jackie Robinson came to Philadelphia with his team to play against the Phillies, he was treated worse here than he was in St. Louis, a place where you always knew you weren't wanted. The Phillies had a manager from Alabama then named Ben Chaplin, who called Robinson all kinds of names and insisted that the players do the same. Dodgers management in New York got wind of this, and I'm sure phone calls were made telling the Phillies leadership they had better get their heads screwed on straight about the matter. So the Philadelphia press came up with a public-relations gimmick, pressuring Jackie to allow photographs to be taken of him shaking hands with Chaplin. At first Jackie wouldn't do it, but he finally consented.

Then, in 1960, the Phillies recruited a black player named Dick Allen. First, he went through their Minor League system before coming to Philadelphia. They sent him to the worst places, such as Arkansas, where a black man could hardly walk down the street. They should have sheltered him from certain areas, but chose to send him there, as if they wanted him to fail. He didn't fail—in fact, he excelled. When Allen went to the Major League team in '64, he was considered their big hitter and named Rookie of the Year—but then he wound up being a scapegoate when the team lost the pennant.

Things like that are why there's been bad blood between the black community and the Phillies since I can't remember. There are some even today who say they'd rather see no baseball at all then watch a Phillies game!

(Just recently, things started to shift for the better. The management changed hands, and Dave Montgomery took over as president. They also hired a black guy named Rob Howard to work in community relations, the job now held by Gene Dias, who's also black and now very involved in the team's programs for local kids.

There must have been some talk among the people who own the ball club, because the Phillies finally invited members of the old Stars and Negro League Baseball Players Association to their events, and agreed to participate in our activities. In the last few years, our relationship has been a lot better, and they've been involved almost continuously with moral and financial support.)

For those few early players, crossing that color line was a huge accomplishment. Yet it took another 12 or 15 years before blacks were fully represented on all Major League teams. In the beginning of integration, there were quotas, so only a handful of black players were hired on any team. In particular, the American League was late in doing that—there were only a few black ballplayers in it until the late 1950s, and the Boston Red Sox waited until the early '60s!

Besides improving the game and revitalizing the sport, integration of Major League Baseball had two other important results. One's a pity, the other's a blessing.

When the Major League teams started to take black ballplayers, that spelled the beginning of the end of the Negro Leagues. The most talented players, especially the young guys with a future, were being bought—poached, really— by the Major League teams. If it meant ignoring contracts they were already signed under, so be it. Once that happened, we started to lose our fan base, because everybody liked to go to Major League ballparks. They figured that's where you were going to see the best.

After the 1947 season, I started wondering if the majors didn't mean to destroy us. The way I looked at it, no matter how well somebody performed in the Minor Leagues, the Major Leagues had no intention of elevating the older players into the big league.

I surely don't regret Jackie Robinson going to the Brooklyn Dodgers or Larry Doby going to the Cleveland Indians. However, if they were only going to bring up a few, then they should not have taken all of our stars. I believe that had they not taken the path they took, the Negro Leagues would have survived.

THE INDIANAPOLIS CLOWNS

In spite of their name, the **Indianapolis Clowns** were not a circus but a baseball team that had their own clowns. The clowns were paid entertainers that traveled with them and put on shows at the ballpark, a little like a mascot at halftime—except they stayed on the sidelines and would act up between innings. It was a special feature of the team, a little added entertainment that would attract an audience and help them make money.

As much as the Homestead Grays traveled, I believe the Indianapolis Clowns had more homes than anyone: Indianapolis, Cincinnati, Buffalo, Charleston, West Virginia, and all other places in between. Where the Clowns did not go, the Homestead Grays had already staked a claim.

The Stars didn't play them often, maybe one or two series a year. The Clowns were a pretty good team, though they couldn't boast any special successes. They did have some solid players from Latin America, and some fine black players from the USA!

Leonard Pigg was one—he was a catcher, like me, and a long-ball hitter. I first met him one winter in 1945 in Chickasha, Oklahoma, when we were both in the Army working at the same hospital. **Felix MacNeil** was a fine shortstop who played in many All Star games.

Then there was **Reece "Goose" Tatum**, who played first base for the Clowns during baseball season and was also a professional player for the Harlem Globetrotters during basketball season.

Buster Haywood was their manager and former catcher. He later helped discover Hank Aaron, baseball's home-run king, when Hank was still playing for a semipro team in Mobile, Alabama.

The Clowns' owners were **Sid Pollack** and **Abe Saperstein**, white Jewish guys who were also big Negro League Baseball promoters. Saperstein owned several basketball teams, including the Globetrotters, and Pollack was involved in all sorts of things in the sports world.

Sure enough, in 1948, the NNL and NAL merged into one league (the NAL), and then they officially disbanded in September 1950. Some of those teams, including the Indianapolis Clowns and Homestead Grays, continued to barnstorm all over the place into the 1960s and even the '70s—but the formal institution of Negro League Baseball was over. A great way of life had ended, and a door closed on a wonderful era.

Integration of baseball not only ended the Negro Leagues as we once knew them, but destroyed the one who made it possible, Jackie Robinson himself. Yet through it all, not once do I recall him embarrassing himself, his family, his friends, or his country.

Eventually, the Dodgers wanted to trade Robinson to the Giants, still in New York at that time. He declined and told them he was retiring. Outwardly, he was still big and strong, a mountain of a man in every way. But inside, there was nothing left. The last time I saw Jackie, his jet-black hair had turned white, and he was suffering from diabetes and high blood pressure. That was the price he paid for being a pioneer. He died in 1972 at 53 years of age, and his widow, Rachel, also a very fine person, had to raise her family by herself.

I'm glad that I was there to know Jackie Robinson personally, and to witness all the things he brought to both black and white America. Baseball is better for it, and our country is better for it. Because after the door of Negro League baseball closed, 100 other doors opened.

Negro League Baseball has done its part to see that the atrocities brought upon blacks in America did not go unnoticed. In fact, the black players who were signed on early to the Major League teams were like ambassadors.

For starters, their presence opened players' eyes to their own ignorance and prejudices. For instance, after Jackie Robinson had joined the Dodgers they played a game against the Philadelphia Phillies. The Phillies had an outfielder named Richie Ashburn who was from a small town in the wilds of Nebraska. At one point, a player named Randy Hammer spiked Robinson on purpose—dug the sharp cleats on the bottom of his baseball shoes into his leg. Richie came running in from center field, and when he saw Jackie bleeding red blood he almost passed out. But Robinson actually wasn't angry with Ashburn. He said, "I realized he didn't know any better."

Think about that: *Richie didn't know Jackie's blood was red.* Ashburn's family had told him nothing about the races and especially black people, and it was news to him. I realize this because he not only turned into one of the finest ball players, but became a good friend. That kind of thing happened all over.

(Then again, that's no excuse. It's only logical Jackie's blood would be red, because I've never seen blood any other color, even from a chicken! And I know they had farm animals out in Nebraska.)

Like I said, Jackie and other pioneers were a dedicated bunch and were playing not just for the money but to raise the standards of black people so we could live better in America. Pro ballplayers had money and position in society, so they proved that success was possible and served as role models for their own people and examples of dignity and accomplishment to everybody else.

These players, and those that went to the Minor Leagues, showed that they were agreeable to meet people and give back to the community by going on speaking engagements, giving autographs to fans, and visiting schools or hospitals and the like. We still do it today, and it has helped us to make a better life for ourselves and also for our own and other families.

What's more, I think integrating the sport had a tremendous impact on promoting civil rights and integration across the country. In fact, I don't believe the segregation laws they passed in the 1950s and '60s made as much of a difference as the acceptance of athletes in America. I daresay Major League baseball has done more for civil rights than the United States Supreme Court! (In case you forgot your history lessons or haven't had them yet, *Brown vs. Board of Education* was a law that desegregated schools in 1954. The Civil Rights Act of 1964 forbids discrimination in all public sectors. Good to know!)

The reason I say this is that a law is just words on a piece of paper. It can't wipe the slate clean if the bad things inside you are still there. Sports are a human thing that everybody loves, and baseball is the great American institution. I don't care if you're young, old, black, white, male or female. When people see great black ballplayers at the stadium or on TV making great plays and winning for their team, maybe even making an error sometimes, it touches them. They see that they're human, and that it's possible for people of different races to work side by side. Everybody has fun and no harm is done. You can't legislate that.

In fact, I would hate to see America yesterday or today or tomorrow without the many sports and sports-related activities life offers us to make ourselves happy. It's a great outlet, for both the athletes and the spectators. Without baseball and sports to entertain us, especially during hard times, I think that you'd see more people jumping off of roofs and bridges.

When I go to speak somewhere now, I like knowing I'll get to see a little kid's face light up hearing about baseball, and meeting me one on one. Afterward, I'll get a dozen letters. I don't know anything better than connecting with others like that.

PART II

After the Leagues

The story of the Negro Leagues doesn't end there—not by a long shot. What black ballplayers did was keep playing ball, those that could. Some went into the majors and went on to set all kinds of records. Others, including yours truly, played in the minors and in Latin America. Still others went into what you might call civilian life. (The Negro League Baseball Players Association now has a list of most of us on its website—www.nlbpa.org. It includes those who made it to the majors, and the couple dozen guys who went into the Hall of Fame.)

Like I said, pretty much all of the Negro League superstars got taken by the majors—Willie Mays, Ernie Banks, Gene Baker, Hank Thompson, Monte Irvin, Don Newcombe, Roy Campanella, Harry Simpson, Jim Gilliam, Minnie Minoso, and so on. Of course, they should've been there all along.

Plenty of others you don't usually hear much about went in, too. For one, Joe Black of the Birmingham Black Barons became one of the Dodgers' greatest relief pitchers. Harry Simpson, from the Philadelphia Stars, was an outfielder who went to the Cleveland Indians.

Then you have people like Judy Johnson of the great old Crawfords team, who became a scout and a coach for the Philadelphia Phillies before he got too old—plus, he was the first black coach in the majors. He scouted for the Milwaukee Braves, too, and one of their players, Bill Bruton, wound up marrying Judy's daughter.

One of the people we can thank for all this is John "Buck" O'Neil, the black former manager and coach for the Kansas City Monarchs. He sent more black guys to the Major Leagues than any other manager. He knew how to bring out your best. Ernie Banks, one of the superior shortstops in Major League history, was his discovery.

Buck got to be coach for the Chicago Cubs, and he traveled all over the place to scout people. Families would call him and he would come and take a look at their sons. He had a great baseball instinct, and if he put his stamp on you, you were going to make it.

Most of the Philadelphia Stars went to the Minor Leagues. I can tell you for sure about some of my buddies. Bill Cash, our other catcher, was in the Chicago White Sox system for a while. Harold Gould joined a provincial league in Quebec, Canada. Wilmer Fields, one of the mainstays of the Homestead Grays, went into the Minor Leagues in Toronto, then later became a parole officer in a facility in Northern Virginia.

Harold Gould

In 1950, it was my turn to move to the minors. Once again, I imagine my story's fairly typical. I got scouted by Honey Russell (who was also a basketball coach at Seton Hall University) and was sold to the Boston Braves organization. I sure wanted to go—the next stop would've been the Major Leagues. At that time they had Johnny Zane and Mark Spot, a relief pitcher named Phil Payne, and another pitcher named Johnson on the team. I just wanted to be around those guys so I could catch them!

First off, the Braves farmed me out to their Minor League team in Hartford, Connecticut, for all of 1951 and '52. That team was fairly young at the time, and was integrated, although there were still just a few black players. It was still small, only 18 men, but I was always a catcher—no more changing positions.

The Hartford Braves were part of the Eastern League, which had teams and played in Hartford; Albany, Schenectady, and Elmira, New York; and Williamsport, Scranton, Allentown, and Wilkes-Barre, Pennsylvania. All of them played schedules of a certain number of games a season and those cities were as far as we'd travel. It was a lot easier—the stops you'd have to make would be within 100 to 200 miles of each other, so we wouldn't be running all over the country like we did in the Negro Leagues. And we no longer rode the bus. Hartford had cars! A fleet of four big old Rios with jump seats behind the front seat and the backseat.

One thing that didn't change was my salary. When I left the Philadelphia Stars, I was up to almost $400 a month. So when I went over to the Braves, I told them, "You have to pay me the same, or I can't stay. I've got a wife at home!" At that time there were ceilings in each league, and you couldn't be paid over a certain amount. So the Minor League teams would pay you up to the figure they could manage and the rest of the money would come from the parent club.

All in all, the living was easier in the Minor Leagues. The thing is, in the Negro Leagues the baseball was better, faster. Mainstream baseball was slower, and there were not as many spectacular players. These guys were solid, but not remarkable. Still, we did have players who went from Hartford right up to the Major League team in Boston, and did very well for themselves. Baseball is a simple enough game, and if you have some ability to play, you'll do all right.

One thing I noticed was that though race relations were better than they had been, they were far from perfect. Like I said, I was one of only a few black men on each of my Minor League teams. I played ball with white guys from Mississippi, Alabama, Tennessee, South Carolina, Georgia. And even after all those years of being side by side on the field and after the games, there was still so much animosity inside some of them. Such people would rather stay ignorant and miserable than be happy. I often ask myself why. It's unhealthy, for both the individuals who are that way and for the people they insult.

Sometimes I'd fight back in small ways. In 1951, I went back to Meridien, Mississippi, for spring training with the Braves organization. We were staying in a motel, and just for spite, I jumped into the pool. The motel management drained it. If I'd jump in three times a day, would they have drained the pool three times a day? They would have gone bankrupt. It just shows you how stupid and costly bigotry can be.

Anyway, after three years with Hartford, I went out to Lincoln, Nebraska for a year, and after that I went out to Quebec City in French Canada. Both of those teams were also part of the Braves organization. And in the wintertime, of course, I went back to the Latin countries.

People sometimes ask me why I didn't wind up in the Major Leagues. It's not by choice. Heck, they said I wasn't good enough. I thought I was, but I had two very fine catchers in line ahead of me, Walker Cooper and Del Crandall, and the Braves weren't about to carry three catchers. But I sure would've gone if I was told to!

I wound up retiring because of an injury to my lower back. Part of my last season I played with a girdle on! And I was getting older—37 or 38. So I said to myself, "I'm not there now, and at this rate I'm not going to get there, so I'd better start looking for something else to do." And I did, and I'm not sorry about that. You can't play forever.

Some people made that decision much earlier, or their situation made it for them. For instance, Max Manning of the Newark Eagles went back to college and got a degree and taught for about 30 years in the school system in New Jersey. Mahlon Duckett of the Philadelphia Stars, who'd had a bout of illness when he was still playing, went to work for the post office as a mailman. Bill Cash eventually went back to the Westinghouse Corporation, where he'd worked during the off seasons.

There were also those who didn't have much money, even after pro careers, so they went back to working for the manufacturing companies that had their own baseball teams. Firms like Westinghouse and GE would hire ballplayers who could no longer play at the top of their form, but could still put in two or three games a week.

Eventually baseball careers came to an end for all, and we went our separate ways, though many of us stayed in touch. Some prospered, but others did not fare well.

After he retired in Atlantic City, John Henry "Pop" Lloyd, who'd played with an early team called the Bacharach Giants, was one who excelled in all facets of life. He used to be a shortstop, and if nothing else is said, all is said. Pop worked for the school system as a custodian, and played for and managed local teams till he was up around 60. He was the Little League commissioner for some time, too.

John Henry was something. He was a complete gentle-man, a Christian, and of course baseball was his game. Everybody loved him, and they've got a park there named after him built way back in 1949. He was a member of the Asbury Park United Methodist Church in New Jersey, where I still have the pleasure of speaking once a year.

Now, of the Philadelphia Stars, Harold Gould has a farm down in Millville, New Jersey, where he owns and trains his own racehorses, and they run all over

New Jersey, Maryland, and Delaware. The late Wilmer Harris worked for a manufacturing company up in Jenkintown, Pennsylvania, and put in somewhere around 35 to 40 years there. I am happy to say that my own life outside of baseball has been most fruitful also. As much as I loved the sport, I found there were more important things in life: the birth of my two children, my wife who cared for them and me, those at church, and the friendships of all who are near me.

Professionally, I moved into the electrical supply business, which I'd gotten into during winters when I wasn't playing ball in Latin America. Now, the skills required for baseball do not in any way coincide with those of wholesale electrical supply! But I got to like it, and I ended up working for three different companies over 42 years: Woodland, Fox, and Ace. I started in receiving, became a counter man, moved to outside sales, and then went into management.

I had a good time and made an awful lot of friends, and became very knowledgeable about the equipment and all the manufacturers. A construction company often works 24 hours a day, so you had to supply three shifts. Whatever the construction companies needed, I found it, so they wouldn't be paying guys $35 an hour to sit down! Whether the item was in Guam or Japan or anywhere, I'd have it shipped that day. It was a lot of running. Even now, some of the big contractors give me a call when they get in a bind, and I'll help them straighten it out and get whatever they need for whatever job they're doing.

During that time, I married again. My marriage to Adele had broken up just as I was getting ready to go into Minor League baseball.

After 12 years together, she suddenly came home one day and said. "You know, Stanley, in about six months when I can save some money, you're going to find me gone." I answered, "Well in that case, you're going to find *me* gone by midnight tonight!" And I left. I don't really know what happened—it wasn't like we'd grown apart because of separation. When the Stars traveled, I took her everywhere with me as much as I could. I guess she just wanted something different.

My second wife, Alberta, was an old friend from our school days and was the mother of my daughter, Lisa. Alberta died from breast cancer when Lisa was five. So, I did the whole house over and raised her by myself, with the help of my mother. Then ma passed away also, and I waited a full five years before I got married again.

I met my third wife, Vera, through my sister Betty—the same one who convinced my family to move north from Virginia. I was on my way to Atlantic

City to visit the boardwalk and have dinner, and Betty asked me if I'd like to bring along some company. When she told me it was Vera, I said, "You mean that skinny little girl who goes to school with your daughter?" But from that night on, we were inseparable. Eventually we started house shopping and moved into a beautiful old four-bedroom home on a big lot in Yeadon, Pennsylvania. And we still live there! I married an angel—the finest female on this planet. If it weren't for the way she's taken care of me all these years, I probably wouldn't still be here.

A year after that marriage, our son Stanley came along, the last male in the Glenn family. I was 48 years old when he was born. As it happened, he is partially deaf in both ears, and the public schools didn't have what it takes to teach him, so we enrolled him in Catholic school with small classes and he did great. It just shows you that if you put in enough damn time, there isn't anything children can't do.

We called Stanley "Chomp" because he was a chow hound when he was growing up. By the time he was in high school at Malvern Prep, he was 6'5" and over 300 lbs. But no baseball for him—he got recruited for football. Eventually he had to quit because he messed up his knee. Turns out, he never really wanted to play—he'd only done it because they'd asked him to.

He graduated from college and law school, and has been a public defender in Florida since he was 25 years old. He's 30 now, quiet and as refined as anyone you'd ever want to know, and married to a country girl from the eastern shore of Maryland.

As for Lisa, she played baseball for fun as a kid and was pretty good herself. She was really something: built like a boy and strong as a mule! She's 43 now and works as an independent businesswoman, selling shea butter and natural personal care-type products for the Abiké Company. Always on the road—she's a little like her dad that way, too.

So neither of my children went into pro sports, but both are interested in my baseball career. As a matter of fact, my son is after me to autograph everything I have now—just in case I kick the bucket before I can do it. Whenever he comes home, he sneaks into the den and rummages around, and after he leaves I notice some of my memorabilia is missing. Well, I think I know where it is!

I have no grandchildren yet. But I've got plenty of kids out there that call me Grandpa Stanley or Uncle Stanley. The love of children makes my heart skip a beat. They are never heavy, but are the real salt of the earth. My services are all theirs.

My service is also devoted to the United Methodist Church, working with the pastors and other ministers of the Conference, to help save souls for God. I'm a certified lay speaker, which means I've taken training to be able to deliver the morning message if the minister is away or needs a break. Usually my message is almost completely religious. But they know I'm a former athlete, and a little bit of baseball usually creeps into what I say!

Yes, my love for baseball is very great, but my love for God is greater. All of us can do both—work and worship—with great success. There's a saying about that: "Render unto Caesar that that is Caesar's, and unto God that that is God's."

Recognition

As you can see, after the Negro Leagues were finished, we all went on with our lives. Of course, we never forgot the experience. But for a long time there—40, 50 years—it seemed the world had forgotten us. There was just nothing out there about it!

Thankfully individual people didn't forget. Sometimes I take a vacation and visit some of the places where I used to play ball. Everywhere I go, there is always someone who remembers. After so many decades, there is something wonderful about that. If any one of these fans reads this book, I want them to know that I love them, too.

Slowly but surely, though, national recognition returned.

Of course, one of the most profound acknowledgments was the induction of Negro League Baseball players into organized baseball's Hall of Fame in Cooperstown, New York. Now, quite a few players got picked after they started playing with Major League teams: Jackie Robinson was the first, back in 1962. I'm talking about when they started putting people in for their contributions during the Negro League Baseball era. That was back in the early '70s when Josh Gibson was still alive.

What had happened was that in the off-seasons, black teams had barnstormed in games against the Major League pros in exhibition games, or in the winter the white players would also go down to Latin America and compete against them. So they got to know that our guys were really super players.

And when a player was picked for the Hall of Fame, likely as not

he'd talk up some of the black players he'd gotten to know, and tell them, "This guy is something."

So that opened the door for some of us to be considered. Of course, there were quotas too on how many black league players the Hall could take in a given year. So you got a situation where someone like Rube Foster—the Father of Black Baseball, for crying out loud—died in 1930 but didn't get put in the Hall till 1981. Fortunately, they finally changed that rule.

Then, in about the late 1980s, memorabilia shows started to become popular, and somebody created Negro League Baseball cards. You know how it is— Americans will always find a way to make money. Those of us players who were still around got invited to the shows and helped stir up a little buzz.

Also, some cities decided it was time to honor their native sons—early players from the great old pre-official teams—and came up with regular holidays for them.

For instance, Judy Johnson, who'd played for the Hilldale Giants and Philadelphia Stars as well as the Crawfords, is from Wilmington, Delaware. Judy, now in the Hall of Fame, had no equal at third base—the closest to him may be Ray Dandridge, also in the Hall. Well, in 1989 the Wilmington Rocks Major League team put up a giant statue of him right in front of their new baseball stadium. (Now, it doesn't favor Judy Johnson at all. And since it was put there on his behalf, I think it ought to resemble him in some form. But it's a statue, and it's the thought that counts!)

Anyway, every year the city holds a festive day to honor him, and the remaining Philadelphia Stars always help to make that day a success, as do the many fine people who attend. Such a huge national celebration is very fitting for a top-notch player like Johnson. A complete gentleman, husband, father, grandfather, and citizen, Judy had a sereneness about him that is not seen in many people in a lifetime. He's one of those people who impact you the first and the last time you are in their presence.

Atlantic City is also proud to honor its own, John Henry "Pop" Lloyd. They have an organization called the John Henry "Pop" Lloyd Committee, and back in 1990 they helped restore the baseball park named after him. Now, every year, they hold a celebration for Pop Lloyd and Negro League Baseball, too. They rent a whole hotel, and we have a big banquet and have a real celebration that lasts four or five days. People from all over America come to this!

These celebrations are precious, because they give all of us ballplayers and our families another opportunity to come together. We always have a great time, and we get to meet old and new fans of all ages.

The Negro Leagues Baseball Museum was also founded in 1990 in Kansas City, by none other than John "Buck" O'Neil. Buck is chairman of the board, though there's a guy by the name of Don Motley who's the CEO and runs the day-to-day show. The museum is quite a place: it shows the history of black baseball from Day One until the present time. They have multi-media displays, memorabilia, photos, and statues of Negro League players. Their store sells everything you can think of to do with Negro League Baseball, and it also has traveling exhibits and some education programs for children. The museum is something wonderful, good, and true. All of America desperately needs to visit to learn about our continuing history.

One person who really got the ball rolling for Buck and his dream of having a great museum was the filmmaker Ken Burns. Burns was working on a huge documentary called *Baseball* that helped put his own name on the map. He interviewed Buck and a couple of the other guys for a section of that film, and they broadcast the whole thing over the course of a week on television in the early '90s.

Ken Burns is a nice guy, and a good businessman. The only thing is, when I met him I had to point something out.

"You know," I said, "in that video you only talk about three teams in the whole Negro Leagues! There were twelve teams, so why show only three?"

He replied, "I just used the things that Buck O'Neil told me."

"Say no more," I said, "because I know Buck!"

The first publicity that came out about *Baseball* was really something. The memorabilia craze, and people wanting to know about Negro League players, really took off after that—and the growth of the museum with it. Why, all kinds of people gave it millions of dollars—especially in the Midwest. The former owners of the Kansas City Monarchs, Tom Baird and Jim Wilkinson, went around and raised money from businessmen and politicians from Missouri and Kansas City and St. Louis, and so on.

With all that help, the museum was able to move from a little office to a huge new complex in the Historic District on 18th and Vine streets. That's near where our teams used to have such a great time when we were in town. Regular folks and celebrities from all over the country and the world have visited, so it does very well financially.

A little bit later in 1990, a fellow named Richard Berg, who's a big music promoter and producer from New York, organized the Negro League Baseball Players Association. It started out to be more of a profit-making thing, but now we're a nonprofit charity.

The purpose of the NLBPA is to honor and celebrate what Negro Leagues players have given to baseball and American history, and to collect and preserve that history, so others can appreciate us for years to come. It's also there to support the players' needs. To be a member, you had to play in the official Negro Leagues between 1920 and 1950.

Once that was set up, we began to get all the guys who could travel and invited them to reunite with us for shows and to support the NLBPA's mission. That also probably had a lot to do with us starting to get noticed again.

Richard Berg was the first president of the NLBPA, even though he wasn't a baseball player (or black, for that matter). But he gave it up after some players tried to sue over commissions on their memorabilia or some such dispute. So then Monte Irvin took over the job. By then, Monte (now in his mid-90s) had gotten into the Hall of Fame and was working for the commissioner of baseball. He didn't like all that traveling as he got older, though, so we got James Jackson, Reggie Jackson's brother, to run the organization. Jackson didn't run it very well. The guy spent the money like it was water. We managed to get him out of there, and then Wilmer Fields took over with me as his first vice president.

Well, after all the trouble we had, we were left with no money, nothing. And then another special person stepped into the picture: Dr. Bob Hieronimus, a Negro League Baseball fan from Maryland whose father-in-law used to be part-owner of the Baltimore Orioles.

One day Bob called us out of the blue, introduced himself, and basically said, "Whatever you need, I've got, and you can have it, and if you ever get so that you can pay it back, fine. If not, that's OK too." Dr. Bob helped us to get an attorney, Charleton Winner, to straighten out our finances and other details, and Fisher and Winner LLC has been the NLBPA lawyer ever since. Dr. Bob has worked very hard to promote everything about Negro League Baseball, and by now, he's just like one of our players!

Bob's quite a guy—he used to be in politics and was the agent of an extraordinary Negro League Player, Leon Day. As a matter of fact, he lobbied the Hall of Fame to put Leon in there where he belonged, and became very close to him before he died. When word came that Leon had been voted in, the old pitcher was lying in St. Agnes Hospital in Baltimore, very ill, and six days later he was gone. That recognition came 50 years too late. Dr. Bob still looks out for Leon's wife, Geraldine, and sees to it she has anything she needs.

Bob and his wife, Zohara, also run 21st Century Radio, a 24-hour network in the Baltimore area. Among other things, they use their radio programs and website to promote Negro League Baseball. He has things set up so one of the former players or their wives or kids can let him know anything new that's happening in that area, and he'll post or broadcast it. And usually at Christmas time, a few of us old players will be guests on his show.

Just this past spring of 2005, the Negro Leagues got their own display in Baltimore. As usual, Dr. Bob Hieronimus was very helpful in making that happen. It's in a sports museum at Camden Station near the ballpark in Camden Yards. This is something that's been about a decade in the making. This small museum will teach the children of America, both black and white, about a part of America they don't really know. This is a good thing, because it will also make it easier for people on the East Coast to learn about us without players having to travel so much to go out and speak.

The NLBPA also got a historian, Todd Bolton. Now, Todd is a man who loves sports, and especially baseball! He has a job with the government of Maryland, but he's always lent his research skills to organizations that promote the sport. He also came to us more or less out of the blue, and volunteered to do whatever he could.

It's an awful lot of work to collect that information, and Todd still doesn't take a penny for it. As a matter of fact, he's also on the Hall of Fame committee, and is one of the people who are going to help pick the next black players who are going to be inducted there. They're holding a special election in 2006, so more of the players from long ago get their shot at it.

Todd is a man I truly believe in and revere. Since we got started, he's traveled thousands of miles to find all the players who played in our heyday. Why, he traveled down to the Latin countries and dug up all the old ballplayers who'd come to America to play with the New York Cubans and some of the other Negro League teams. His findings are as complete as possible and are truly authoritative.

What's more, Todd is like a little brother to me, and his lovely wife, Judy, and their two sons are like family. (Judy's a dickens. If she sees me half a block a way and I'm smoking a cigarette, she'll come right over, yank it out of my mouth, and kiss me. She'll say, "That should take care of *that*!" She's been ill lately, so you can bet I make sure to check in on her often.)

People like Dr. Bob and Todd truly care about the fate of the league, the players, and preserving our legacy. Pretty soon more and more folks started to come aboard and help us. And everything started to snowball.

I knew we were really starting to take our rightful place when Dr. Bob Hieronimus arranged for me (along with Mahlon Duckett, Gene Benson, Bill Cash, Russell Awkard, Jim Cohen, Wilmer Fields, Max Manning and Leon Day) to meet then-President Bill Clinton. Clinton's my guy—as far as I'm concerned, he's the finest president this nation ever had.

I still remember the date: February 16, 1994. The President got called away, but Vice President Al Gore met us and stayed with us the whole time. We spent at least three or four hours touring the White House, with escorts who took us all over the place. We even got to go into the room where all the decisions are made—but not allowed to sit in the chairs! (It's OK—no one gets to do that.)

Vice President Gore was most hospitable, and spoke to us at length about the Negro League and Willie Mays in particular. When he was young, Gore saw Mays when he was just starting to play in the League. He asked us a lot of questions, and we were pleasantly surprised that he knew of so many of our guys. But of course, Tennessee is Gore's home state, and Negro League teams had played in Memphis, home of the Memphis Red Sox, and Nashville, where the Baltimore Elite Giants originated.

The photos we made of us shaking hands are priceless to me, and I shall keep them always. You won't be surprised to know I was very angry when he didn't make it as President in 2000! (By the way, I did get to shake hands with Mr. Clinton later—at a baseball celebration in Washington, D.C.)

Many other invitations from governments and schools have come our way over the last decade. Among others, the New York State Legislature, Cheyney University (the oldest historically black college in America), Fairfield College prep school, and the Urban League of Youngstown, Ohio, invited many of us former players to visit and speak. All of them left nothing unturned in honoring us. My den is now graced with a large plaque from the New York Assembly, a Hall of Fame achievement award from Cheney, and a gold key to the city of Youngstown. (Just recently, I myself was inducted into Eastern Shore Baseball Hall of Fame in Salisbury, Maryland, near where I was born.)

A bigger milestone recognizing black players, and acknowledging the days of segregation, was when they established Jackie Robinson Day. In 1997, for the 50th anniversary of his signing with the Dodgers, Jackie's wife Rachel published a book and the federal government passed an act to mint a silver dollar in his honor. Then a couple of years ago, Bud Selig, the commissioner of Major League Baseball, took that a step further. He declared that every year, April 15 would be Jackie Robinson Day all over the Major Leagues and in all the ballparks. So now everybody has to celebrate that fact, and nobody can skip out. Yes, that order came down from Major League Baseball itself!

The Phillies have invited the Philadelphia Stars to celebrate the day with them each year, so we get to go to their ballpark. All we really do is watch the game and eat and drink, but we have a good time. It's like that all over the country, and it's a great remembrance. Nothing that we do will really measure up to the great one, but they're learning!

Before I close this chapter, I can't forget to mention all the public schools, libraries, Philadelphia's Germantown Historic Society, WDAS with Tamlen Henry and WHAT with Johnny Sample, Congressman Chaka Fattah, and Governor Ed Rendell of Pennsylvania for their support over the years. Whatever the Philadelphia Stars do, we know we can count on them. I hope they read this book, because I want them to know how much I appreciate them.

The Brotherhood Continues

A way of life is gone now, and most of us are gone also. There are fewer than 70 Negro League players still remaining. By now, we're all retired, not just from baseball but from working altogether.

We live far and wide, but like I said, Negro League Baseball is like a fraternity, and frat brothers are all for one and one for all. It doesn't make any difference that we aren't playing baseball together any more. We're a bunch of old guys who have withstood each other all these years, and it shows when we're around together that we genuinely like each other.

Though each of us is 70-plus, we still love to see good sights, eat good food, and enjoy nature's wonders. Our families know each other, and our children are with us when we promote shows and when we are asked to appear someplace.

Why, Buck O'Neil is about 95 years old now and still has all his marbles. As a matter of fact, I saw Buck when I went out to Kansas City in the fall of 2004 to make a video. The way he treated me, it was as if it had only been a week since we were together, and I wound up staying an extra day. If you ever go up there and tell him Stanley Glenn sent you, see if doesn't give you anything you want!

Of the men who remain, the Philadelphia contingent is a tight-knit group. Usually a few of us travel together, and you should hear our conversations. How we talk! We go on and on about our spouses, and we express with glee the success of our children and grandchildren and exult in each other's triumphs.

In fact, Mahlon Duckett, Harold Gould, and Bill Cash and I are like blood brothers. We've seen each others' children get born and watched them grow up and graduate from college and have kids of their own. There are members of my real family I'm not as close to.

Hal Gould is down in Millville New Jersey, and Bill Cash is here in West Philadelphia. Mahlon Duckett, who also lives in Philadelphia, is now closer to me than the other ball players because his wife and their children and I have known each other for 64 years. We were the youngest members of the Stars. In fact, there's not a day goes by that Mahlon and I don't talk.

So we all stay fairly close to each other. And if somebody needs some help, we do it if it's humanly possible. For example, Mahlon's wife, Beatrice, passed recently. She was a very fine person. At her memorial last summer, we had a full house. Of course, the Duckett family is huge; Mahlon alone has seven daughters. To show you how people loved her, there were enough bouquets there for Philadelphia not to have to buy any more flowers for a week!

I'm also still close to all the guys I played sports with at Bartram High School, where my baseball career began. As of now, there are 12 of us still living. I'm the only black guy there, and the oldest except for one, Steve Rollo. Every seven or eight weeks we go to lunch at Lehmann's restaurant out in Essington, Pennsylvania. Usually it takes us about three-and-a-half hours to eat. Now, you know it doesn't take that long to chew a sandwich. We linger because we're always reminiscing about the things we did in the '40s.

It was during one of those lunches that I finally found out about the Yankees scouting me, then turning tail and going home after they found out my race.

We were sitting there cutting up and having fun and suddenly Steve said, "Stan, did anybody ever tell you that the Yankees came to see you?"

I said no. "Well, there was some talk, but I didn't believe it."

"It's true, Stan," he said. "I was there."

I laughed. "Shame on them. They missed out. I didn't."

It turns out that at the time our coach, Mr. Goldblatt, wouldn't let them tell me, and they'd kept it a secret all those years. They said they thought it was going to hurt my feelings. But they could do nothing about it; that was how the times were. It just goes to show you what kind of friendship we've had, that they just told me a few years ago. They're great guys.

Normally, the rest of us from the different Negro League teams meet at least once a year at some reunion, and some of us spend a lot of our time helping out with the Negro League Baseball Players Association—especially me! Right now,

Mahlon Duckett and Bill Cash are the secretary-treasurer and vice president, respectively, and Harold Gould is on the board of directors.

How I got to head the thing is succession. The former president, Wilmer Fields, was there from about 1993 until he died last June, so I moved into the presidency. I figured I'd take the job because I'm the youngest of the whole group, and I might have a little bit more to offer than some of the others. Especially the older guys—they have a harder time getting around. That, and if I *hadn't* taken it, Wilmer might've come up out of the grave and given me a talking to!

We do keep busy. My job description is: I do everything. The organization itself has my home phone number as its own. I don't have a secretary, but my wife, Vera, is home most of the time and we keep the answering machine hooked up. I might go out for a while, and when I come back I'll have 10 or 15 messages from former players and people related to Negro League Baseball. I answer them all as soon as possible, just in case something is wrong or they need something that we can provide.

I'd like to tell you about some of the things we do for one another. One is keep track of everybody and make sure they're informed about what's going on. Recently I asked our historian, Todd Bolton, to send me an up-to-date roster of all the players who are living so I can write to them a couple of times a year and send them information about what we're doing that they otherwise would not know. We should meet every month, and I always like as many of the guys as possible to come. We haven't met in quite a while lately, but we're always on the phone with one another.

Our organization is always trying to build our finances so very needy former players can have some assistance from within. Many Negro League veterans are living sub-standard existences, but some are too proud to ask for help. Few are bitter, though, and that pleases me. People do come forward all the time—even people that never played, such as wives and other relatives. We do whatever we can for them, and it's always going to be *something*.

Of course, we're not a rich organization. We depend on donations and in that we've been fortunate. There's one fellow whose name I won't reveal who gives us $10,000 a year. Checks come in from all over the country for several hundred dollars at a time. We want to get Corporate America to help the Players' Association, which to my knowledge it has not yet done. We would also like to hear from generous individuals who would like to contribute.

I don't know of any individual Major League team that gives the NLBPA money. Of course, Major League Baseball already does have its Baseball

Assistance Team, which sees to it that ballplayers who have fallen on hard times get help with finances or their medical problems. A former Negro League player, Joe Black, was one of the founders of that program. Thanks in part to him, Major League Baseball now provides pensions to some of us former players.

Joe, who passed in 2002, was a kind and caring man and a great friend, to me as well as to those in dire straits. No warmer person have I ever met. Yet no one dared lie to him, because he'd instantly get angry. Thanks to him, the BAT organization has been a real force for the destitute and the dying, including those from Negro League Baseball. That's a good thing.

We have lost so many these past few years. We recently paid respects to our oldest guy, Double Duty Radcliffe, who was 103. It was all over the news, because he was the oldest living professional baseball player! He made his home in Chicago, and I used to see him two or three times a year.

We buried Max Manning about four years ago. He was quite a guy. His oldest daughter, Linda, and I are very close. She's a member of the John Henry "Pop" Lloyd Association, which does an awful lot for kids and promoting baseball, so we still see each other five or six times a year.

Wilmer Harris passed on two days before Christmas 2004. I call his family often—it's been over a year now, but I miss him like he was just here yesterday.

These days, we might have three or four deaths a month. And of course, as NLBPA president, I should be there at as many funerals as possible, and send flowers and donate sums of money if we can. All in all, we do a pretty good job of taking care of each other.

On a happier note, the Players Association also has promoters, especially on the East Coast. (I don't usually travel farther west than Kansas City these days.) We typically stage six or eight memorabilia shows a year. Demand is pretty high, so that a collector or player can sell a 3-x-5 photo for anywhere from $4 up, and 8 x 10 pictures usually go for ten dollars apiece. Baseballs that are signed by multiple players might be worth $100 to $150.

Besides baseball players, these shows sometimes bring in the old football players, too. Every time we have a show in Washington, D.C. or Chantilly, Virginia, it seems like half of the Redskins team will come in. We've gotten to know each other well, and we always have a good time.

I'd like to take along some more of our remaining players to the memorabilia shows so that they can get a few hundred dollars in their pockets, too. But only about a dozen of those left can travel. We have a couple in California, and not all can do things well by themselves, so when we bring them East we sometimes have to arrange for a relative to come along and help. We do what we can to pay for it and make the arrangements. Now, that's real closeness.

On top of all this, we go to some of the Fan Fests put on by Major League Baseball as publicity for their All Star games. They like ballplayers to go to these events because it draws lots of fans who come and buy things.

For example, in 1996, the baseball Fanfest was held in Philadelphia. We hosted the All Star game, at which I made many friends. I also have to say that the Negro League display there was fantastic. I guess we were really starting to become famous again, because on my way to breakfast at the Marriott Hotel, a half block away, some 200 kids descended on me at the door for autographs. I missed breakfast, but the looks on their faces more than made up for it. We lined them up along the side of the hotel, being careful not to block the door, and signed whatever they had for free.

That sort of thing keeps us in the public eye, so people will always remember us and become interested in our history and players.

Of course, sometimes at these promotional events you run into people from the old days, and it gives you a little perspective.

Double Duty Radcliffe used to be a big draw at these memorabilia shows. He was something. People just gravitated to him because he was funny, and you might say he had a vivid imagination. It could get to be 11 or 12 o'clock at night, and Duty would still be sitting there in the lobby talking, surrounded by 100 people. And he was 100 years old at the time! Now, most of his stories *could* be true. I wouldn't know, because it all happened before I came along. But I'd been listening to his same stuff for 60 years, so when I'd walk in and see Radcliffe, I'd say "Uh-oh!" and turn around the other way.

I've also run into a white Major League player and Hall of Famer by the name of Enos "Country" Slaughter a number of times at card shows and such. In the 1940s and '50s, Slaughter was an outfielder for the St. Louis Cardinals, among other teams. At one point, he tried to convince all the players on the Cardinals not to report to the ballpark because they'd have to face a certain black guy named Jackie Robinson when they played the Dodgers. That was hateful.

Yet here it was years later and I'd be at a memorabilia event and every place we'd go you'd look up and Slaughter would be hanging with our team. So I finally asked him how he'd become so comfortable with black ballplayers.

"Slaughter," I demanded, "I can't understand you. Every time I turn around I'm stepping on your feet. You couldn't stand me thirty years ago."

He looked at me and said, "You know, you're right, Stan. I was dumb. I learned better!"

I said, "Enos, I can't take that for an answer because you're from the Carolinas and you've been around black folks all your cotton-pickin' life!" But that's the way he let it slide, and I even grew to like him a little bit, too.

Anyway, another of the big things the NLBPA does is sends us players out for public speaking at schools and universities, churches and civic groups and such. Ours is such a great history that my goodness, somebody has to tell it, so that the schools can teach it, and all people will know we existed. Even with Black History Month and all these promotions and shows we do, 99 out of 100 children that we speak to—and their mothers and fathers—still don't know about Negro League baseball.

Usually I give the kids a sort of classroom lesson—tell them when Negro League Baseball got started, how many teams were in the League, how many players for thirty years represented Negro League Baseball—everything from the color of the uniforms to guys who hit home runs 600 feet. And I always brag about my two children and my wife, and I tell them it's been a very good life.

I do tell them about the hardships we went through, but not the really terrible stuff, because a lot of things stay with children for a long time. I don't want to put something scary in a child's head that I don't personally think should be there. So if books don't tell the story as it was, that's not my fault. I'll usually say that yes, it was bad, you couldn't eat out, you couldn't go to the theater, sometimes you couldn't buy gasoline, and sometimes you were afraid for your life. But I don't really mention the Ku Klux Klan.

When it's over, I make sure that I have 30 minutes to an hour to answer all questions from children and their families and anybody else in the audience. Most of the time, everybody asks about the famous and familiar names—Satchel Paige, Josh Gibson, Jackie Robinson. Kids want to know how many home runs this one hit, what is this one's batting average and things like that. I tell them from the beginning that I cannot answer precisely. And what's more, that there's no one else alive who can tell them, either.

They say to me, "But Mr. Glenn, I've seen some statistics in books." And I say, "They're lies!"

Then I give them my phone number and address and say, "If you're writing term papers or book reports at school, and you need some help or want to know something, call me. Or if you don't want to speak over the phone, you can come by my house." A lot of them take me up on it, and I assure them they're not only welcome but tell them to bring their friends. We sit in my den and I answer every question they can think of.

So, slowly but surely, our story is coming into the schools. But one student writing a paper will do nothing to put it into a history book, something more permanent that they'll have to study if they go to school. Getting this information into libraries is the only way to prevent this part of American history from being lost when the few players still alive are gone.

But you know, I'm not just trying to inform these kids. I want to inspire them and help them to realize the future is theirs. For example, a few months back I spoke to seventh graders in Linwood, New Jersey, near Atlantic City. I told them, "In ten years you're going to be out of school and you and other kids like you all over America are going to be running this country. And I want to tell you that I think the country is in good shape." You should've seen the smiles I got from that. Their faces just lit up.

Then I told them, "There's plenty of news on TV, the newspapers are full, so don't just turn to the comics every time. Try reading some of the other stuff—especially the editorials." At that, I got a bad, "I-don't-want-to-know-about-that" type of look.

I talk to kids this way wherever I go because I want them to know that I believe in them. They need all the encouragement they can get, what with the things that happens on the streets today—children raising children, no man in the house, eight-year-olds being shot at and killed.

I'll say, "If the president of the United States says something and you know it's not true, you don't have to vote for him! You've got minds of your own when you're old enough." And if anybody asks me my opinion on current events, I'll go ahead and tell them just like it is. By the time kids are in seventh grade and ask you a question, they don't want a half-answer. They want honesty from someone who they believe knows what he's talking about. And they can see through you quicker than *you* can see through you!

I tend to speak my mind when I talk at gatherings of adults, too, at various public places. I always have plenty to say about Negro League Baseball, but that's not my only topic. We'll talk about politics and current events. It's all related.

And when I do, sometimes I think things haven't changed much when it comes to race, especially in the South.

For instance, I travel down to Richmond in my home state of Virginia about twice a year for card shows and other baseball promotions. Virginia was part of the Confederacy, of course, and to this day standing outside this one building they've got a huge statue of a stallion with General Robert E. Lee on its back. This is the guy who basically fought to save slavery.

One night I was giving a speech there and couldn't help but mention the statue. "You've been honoring him since the Civil War," I pointed out. "and I know that you like him. Yet you had a black man, Arthur Ashe, one of our finest tennis players in the world. Somehow you couldn't find a place to put up a monument for him. Why is that?"

That was infuriating enough. And the next thing I said I know I shouldn't have, but I did it anyway. "What we should have done to Robert E. Lee is convened a court martial. He should have been found guilty and had his behind put in jail!"

Well, the audience wanted to kill me! Usually, when I've finished a talk I allow about a half-hour for questions and answers. That night, they hustled me right out of there. They even had to call the state police to escort me!

I had one friend in the audience, though. Earlier that evening, I'd met a boy named John, about 13 or 14 years of age, who'd come with his parents. He was a big baseball fan and I gave him a signed baseball and some pictures. We really hit it off, and I could've done anything down there and he would have stood by my side!

He wrote me later to thank me and mentioned the hubbub: "My mom and dad didn't teach me like that, so don't be too hard on us!" John's a grown man now, but I still get letters from him several times a year. He's my buddy.

Baseball Today

One thing I always do now that I'm retired is watch television every night when there's a baseball game on, and I still go to live games whenever I can. My friends and I sit around watching and they say, "Stan, what happened there? The poor guy just doesn't know, he just doesn't have the ability to really do it."

I have to agree. Not only are the Negro Leagues gone, but baseball just isn't what it used to be, period! As far as I can see, today we have a Major League in name only. The quality is not there. Three-quarters of the fellows in the American and National leagues today couldn't make it into Triple-A ball 40 years ago.

How can that be? For starters, ballplayers are not as physically fit as they used to be, even though they have everything at their disposal to get themselves in shape. Major League teams all have excellent places for you to come and work out in the winter time, where you can get any medical attention that you need. But instead, some of them use steroids.

They always had them back in the day, but guys didn't use them like they do today. They didn't need them! They had great bodies because they had had a tough time coming up. In the neighborhood where I grew up, you could play baseball in the street if you didn't have a field nearby, and you didn't have to worry about cars coming around and running over you because there were only five autos in a two-mile radius.

But the real problem is that the talent is spread so thin. During the time of the Negro Leagues, we had 16 Major League teams, and in those you had the very best ball players in the country. Now there are about 30 teams, and baseball is watered down. Too many people, not enough talent.

In the beginning, St. Louis was as far west as the Major Leagues went. At one point we had three Major League Baseball teams in New York: the Yankees, the Giants, and the Brooklyn Dodgers. Only the Yankees were making money. So, the other two teams were looking for greener pastures. And the Los Angeles area was that package.

Los Angeles is home to a lot of Hispanic people from Mexico. They have always played baseball in their country and they love it. So the owners knew that they were going to get an influx of people of Mexican descent trying out, and people from all parts of the country that were big on baseball—namely Southerners and black folk. The Dodgers and the Giants had had black players from early on, and they knew that they were going to be able to scout more out there.

So baseball started to spread out, and people were either starting new teams out West, where they thought they could drum up some new players and fans, or they were looking for a buyer so they could get rid of a losing team. That's what happened to the Philadelphia Athletics. They were not drawing too well, and the owner, Connie Mack, was a nice man who'd been in baseball all of his life but couldn't afford to keep them. So they went to Kansas City for a while, then they were sold again and wound up in California.

Eventually there were teams all up and down the West Coast—Los Angeles, San Diego, San Francisco, Seattle. And because they extended baseball by twice the size it was originally, we don't have enough players to stack those teams. So they have put the next-best out there, and the caliber of baseball is just not as good as it was 30 years ago.

On top of that, it just got to be so expensive to own a team that after a while only the richest could. Back then, if the owners wanted or needed a new ballpark, they would have to pay part of the price to build it. (Not like today, where the taxpayers foot most of the bill.) So the only people who could afford teams were those with more money than they knew what to do with, and who didn't mind throwing it around. And soon, instead of team pride and supporting baseball for its own sake, the sport became a commodity.

There's another side to it too. Until the 1960s, baseball was a game where once you signed a contract, you belonged to that team and that owner for the rest of your life, or till they didn't want you anymore. Then here comes Curt Flood, a black center fielder for the St. Louis Cardinals, who took a stand. A real good player and no dummy, Curt got traded from St. Louis to the Philadelphia Phillies. And Curt refused to come to Philadelphia because of the way they had treated Jackie Robinson.

Well, you couldn't tell people in baseball what you were or weren't going to do. But Flood put his foot down, and the trade didn't go through. So he got black-balled, and never played another Major League game. And he was one of the four or five best center fielders in baseball!

(As a matter of fact, Flood died about five years ago. Do you know how many people were at his funeral? Four or five. That's terrible, and goes to show you how people in baseball no longer care about each other the way we used to.)

Now, it wasn't fair that signing a paper to play baseball was like signing a marriage license. Curt Flood helped open the door for ballplayers to have some rights, and made it possible for people to get better deals and not get stuck for 10 or 15 years in one place unless they wanted to. So then the unions got involved, and collective bargaining came in, and now you only need to stay in an organization for five years.

But unions also led to Major League baseball salaries being where they are—crazy, in the millions. And once those unions and profit sharing and so forth came into the picture, it made relationships more difficult from the days where you'd just sign and play.

Because of all this, baseball has ceased to be a sport. And why? Because the almighty dollar came in and dictated. Now it's a money-making machine, like any other investment. Baseball has become *A Rich Man's Game.*

Years ago families used to own teams, and I liked it more then. Some were former players, and most were in it just because they loved baseball. And I don't think anybody loves it today like they did 60 or 70 years ago.

Now everything is owned by big conglomerates. There are very few privately owned teams anymore, because like I said, if you're not a billionaire you can't afford to own one. And believe me, half the time these owners don't know as much about baseball as my cap does! It's like a hobby to them.

George Steinbrenner owns the New York Yankees. But he also owns a shipping fleet and his home is actually in Tampa, Florida. He can do anything he wants to, and hire whomever he wants to, because he has all the conglomerates and whatnot at his feet.

We have people in American baseball now who are not even Americans. Rupert Murdoch is a media tycoon from Australia. He owns the Dodgers today.

I don't think Murdoch knows the difference between a baseball and a football. Branch Rickey must be turning over in his grave!

Because there's big money involved, the whole thing has become very political. For example, I believe that the Major Leagues had to pay Baltimore Orioles owner Peter Angelos a certain amount of money for him to allow them to build another ballpark within 35 miles of Baltimore. This is another guy who has more money than he knows what to do with already.

Now, Baltimore has plenty of people, and their games are sold out most of the time. So why would Angelos even want to block the National League from putting a Major League team in Washington? There *is* some baseball policy about location. But I understand from the grapevine that there are about 100 law firms along the Eastern Seaboard, and Angelos "owns" all of them—never mind whose name is actually on their door.

Even the steroid scandal you see today is about money. *Finally* last spring they had a session in Washington, D.C. with the heads of all the major sports to discuss how they're going to standardize the rules about drug use and testing. Well, if they hadn't been so gung ho to get that dollar, they would've taken care of this a dozen years ago. It would've been done without the fanfare and the United States Congress coming into it. But they overlooked the doping and did nothing till it got out of hand.

Baseball today is also gouging the fans. The sport makes its money from those who can afford to buy box seats. And parking will probably cost you $20 unless you have a superbox. They're also building new stadiums smaller, because they don't want to have any grandstands or bleachers like they used to in the wonderful old days, filled with regular fans and kids on a Saturday afternoon. They want corporations to buy the superboxes so they can get money years in advance.

It's a shame. How often can a regular guy afford to take himself and his wife and his children to a ballgame? Maybe a couple of times a season. If it's going cost you $200, that might be a third of the mortgage payment on your house.

Actually, they make more money off memorabilia than they do from selling tickets. And at every ballpark now, each team has its own stuff for sale. For instance, you can go down to the new stadium in Philadelphia and buy shirts, hats—practically an entire wardrobe. They've got so many retail stores in there it's like a shopping mall. "Ashburn Alley" is open hours before the park opens so that people can come in and eat, drink, do all their Christmas shopping, and the game doesn't even start until 7:05! It's going to be their downfall, if you ask me.

You know what else is sad? The sport is now integrated, but there actually aren't that many black players these days. About 25 years ago, about 69 percent of the players in the Major Leagues were black. Now it's less than 12 percent. That's a pretty big drop and it's not because they couldn't play if they wanted to. It's because black kids just don't play baseball any more.

In my little town, Yeadon, we have two athletic facilities, but you seldom see kids out there playing. There must be five baseball fields at the new development at 70th street and Lindberg Boulevard in Southwest Philadelphia, but I have only seen *one* game going on in the last five years!

At all of the schools that I speak to, I always ask the black children why they don't play baseball. They tell me "I play basketball," or football. Then I ask them *why* they don't want to play baseball, and they don't know.

So I tell them, "Look, even if you get lucky enough or good enough to make the NBA, by the time you're 30 years old you're going to be a cripple. Even Michael Jordan really only had about 12 years, and retired young. Same with football. I don't care who you are or how strong you are, we're all made out of the same stuff. Those sports are so demanding that by the time you're finished with it, it's for the rest of your life.

"Whereas, I was in baseball and caught for 20 years. As a matter of fact, I've known baseball players, like Satchel Paige, who peaked at 40 years old, and older!

"Look at me today," I say, "I'm almost 80 and I'm still in good shape." But it seems to go over their heads.

To be sure, there's still racism in baseball. For example, in the spring of 2005, I went down to Maryland to help a group of black investors from Memphis who wanted to buy the Washington Nationals. They were looking for someone to speak to the city council on their behalf, and I told them it would be an honor. The possibility is very exciting to me, so I have given them advice and even wrote a letter to Commissioner Bud Selig. As the president of the Negro League Baseball Players Association, I have a little bit of influence there.

This group has put an offer on the table that exceeds that of anyone else for the last year and a half. They have met every criterion they'd been asked to meet. Yet there's still no deal. My group even said they'll build their own stadium, which will cost something like $766 million dollars. If these people can raise enough money for a billion-dollar empire, why do you suppose someone still won't sell it to them? It's because they're black, and no other reason.

It's like they say: The more things change, the more they stay the same. Even right here in Philadelphia, they really only want one or two black players on the

Phillies team. Dave Montgomery, who is the cornerstone of the Phillies, is a fine man, but it's still a neighborhood thing in this city, and there are some people and places that don't want blacks around at all! Yes, even today.

I have a few ideas on how to make it better. Let's begin with the Office of the Commissioner. The commissioner shouldn't be a team owner, because that's a conflict of interest. Get a man or woman to run the office independently, on behalf of baseball. Run it not for the best interests of the owners or players, but for the sport. Sounds corny, doesn't it?

Commissioner Bud Selig is the owner of the Milwaukee Braves. Supposedly, he gave the ballclub to his daughter to run. But whatever they tell you, Bud Selig is still in charge of the Milwaukee Braves and she is just a figurehead. It goes to show you that they want somebody in the commissioner's job who is going to do what the owners want, so they can keep on doing their flim-flam.

We should bring back somebody like Fay Vincent, who was commissioner until 1992, when he was forced out. Fay Vincent is one of the champions of black guys from the Negro Leagues getting into baseball and receiving hospitalization and pensions. If Vincent had been commissioner when the steroids thing came up, he would have squashed it then and there, because baseball was his main priority. Of course, he wanted the owners to make money—they *have* to in order to stay in business. But he would have run the system so that when this crap cropped up, he would've taken care of it. Well, he was too true, too much of a baseball man. And that's why they got rid of him.

Baseball has also gotten away from placing younger people in managerial jobs. They tend to go with the older fellows, but it would be more exciting if they hired younger guys, because they simply have more upstairs. Older people sometimes don't have the ideas or presence of mind that exists in younger people. I watch the youngsters in Philadelphia play some of the same games we played when I was a kid—yet altogether differently, because they will invent something new. Baseball needs their spark in its leadership.

The Stars' Landmark

Major League Baseball sure has changed, but these days Negro League Baseball is coming alive again, and my home city of Philadelphia is taking some small steps to regain its reputation as a baseball mecca.

You'd figure sooner or later the Philadelphia Stars had to get something special of their own, and finally we did. In 1998, here in Philadelphia, a gal named Christen Langdon saw a documentary about Negro League Baseball and got fired up about making our name more known and helping the players, especially the Philadelphia Stars.

Christen had worked in Ed Rendell's office when he was mayor, then went to work for the *Philadelphia Tribune*, so she knew how to get things done. Heck, sometimes she'd get a little ahead of herself, but it was all good. In time, a marker and a sign commemorating the leagues was installed over at the corner of Belmont and Parkside avenues.

Then, in 2002, the Business Association of West Parkside stepped in. They wanted to help the neighborhood economy and thought it would be a good idea to develop that corner some more by turning it into a tourist destination. Marjorie Ogilvie and Miller Parker, who are local real-estate developers, started working with the community groups and the city offices and such to put up a larger-than-life bronze statue there honoring the Negro Leagues, because we were the local heroes! I was excited about that.

They started raising money, and got the government agencies and the Phillies on board. Then Miller and Marjorie got in touch with each of us former Stars to tell them the names of the ballplayers that lived in this area, and proposed to get baseballs and bats so we could sign them to help raise money for all the good things they wanted to do.

All of the remaining Stars got together with everyone and collaborated in the whole process on what the statue should be like. As it happens, the guy who made the statue, Phil Sumpter, is a graduate of John Bartram High School, although he's younger so I didn't know him.

Now, when I finally saw the statue, I thought, "It doesn't look like any one of us who'd played." I heard it might be modeled on Josh Gibson, but it doesn't resemble him in any way. But again, it's a statue, and I like it well enough!

The unveiling took place down at Veterans Stadium in 2003, and we were there. It felt good to see it, real good. Of course, you could say it was nice to be acknowledged, but then again we were recognized here in Philadelphia a long, long time ago. At that time the Phillies pledged money to care for it over the next 10 years, and since then they have contributed very, very handsomely to the park project there.

The thing is, we still needed an awful lot of money to make the whole corner come together. So I and the Philadelphia Stars and Miller and Marjorie went around to all of the unions here in the city of Philadelphia to see if we could get them on board with the project. The workers needed to see that we actually exist—that we are real people! It took some time to travel around like that, but they met us and we signed autographs and gave them pictures, and pretty soon they said, "We'll do the work." For free! Now what could be better than that?

Once that was set, the park's sponsors threw a black-tie benefit ball at the Mann Music Center in the fall of 2004. Why, everyone was there—politicians, celebrities, business people, and community leaders. The Philadelphia Phillies were well represented also. The owners and the general manager and some of the players attended, and the president of the organization, Dave Montgomery, made a very nice speech.

The workmen started to build the park in the beginning of 2005, and as they were working I noticed the union guys started to get interested in and excited about black baseball. Some of them even told me they'd found out that they had relatives who'd played in the Leagues.

Every chance I got, I'd ride by there and stop and watch them work. Some would ask me questions about back in the day—all the natural things such as players' names and "How'd you like playing here, or there?" Of course, they also wanted signatures and baseballs and other memorabilia. I told them, "Whatever you want, you're going to get!" Why not: I'm so in debt to the unions of the city who have done most of this work for us for nothing!

Well, finally they got what is now called the Philadelphia Stars Negro League Memorial Park and statue to the point where they were ready to dedicate it. Of course, the date they picked was April 15, 2005—Jackie Robinson Day.

And on that day, there I was with the last living members of the Philadelphia Stars being honored with Jackie for our own contributions to the sport. When Mahlon Duckett, Hal Gould, Bill Cash, Wilmer Harris's son, and I showed up at the Philadelphia Business and Technology Center, there was a fancy horse-drawn carriage waiting to take us up to the staging area. Of course we climbed in and trotted up Parkside Avenue to where a good-sized audience was waiting, along with politicians, civic leaders, bureaucrats, and some of the Phillies were up on a stage. Gene Dias, the Phillies' director of community relations, was emceeing. After we got seated everyone made speeches congratulating us.

When it was my turn at the mike, I talked about losing Wilmer, how proud I was to be a ballplayer, and how we spend most of our time sharing the story of black baseball. Of course, I made a point to mention how the last living Stars have been friends for so long; we're like family—probably closer.

After they set the statue in place, we autographed our portraits, posed for pictures, and told our sports tales to the reporters. (Sometimes when we speak to the press, we start to stretch things a little bit. So I say. Woah, let's tell the truth— it was a great time full of amazing moments, and we don't *need* to stretch them!)

Later, at the Carousel House in Fairmount Park, we had hot dogs, signed more autographs for the kids all after-noon, and talked with old friends who'd dropped by from out of town.

What could be better? That day I felt happy and, frankly, completely surprised. I know my teammates enjoyed it also.

Later that evening we went to the Phillies-Braves game at Citizens Bank Park. We ran out onto the field, where the Phils honored Jackie Robinson and us again. The Tuskeegee Airmen and Miss Black Pennsylvania were out there too. Then we climbed up into our warm box seats with an eagle's eye view of the field, where they fed us all kinds of food and beer. The guys were chowing down and cutting up, but as I sat there remembering Jackie, I got a bit wistful about what happened to him, having to suck up all that hostility in the beginning.

I said, "You know, that's why he's not here anymore. There's only so much the body can take, whether it's physical or mental. Sooner or later, something is going to break." I just wish he could have been there celebrating in the box with us. No doubt he was, in spirit.

A couple months after we dedicated the statue and the Philadelphia Stars Negro League Memorial Park, the whole thing was nearly complete. You should come see it: granite walls inscribed with the names of all of the Stars players' names and the names of all the teams in the Negro Leagues. Green landscaping, lights, the works.

Across the street on the corner there's a huge mural with bold colors showing us in action. It was created through the auspices of the Mural Arts Program of Philadelphia. The fellow that painted it, David McShane, has done murals all over the world. He's quite a guy. He's about as big as my little finger! But he knows what he's doing, and as long as he's doing something good, I'm going to be right in his corner.

As a matter of fact, that mural and park on the corner have already had an effect on the neighborhood and communities nearby. For example, I go to church just about every Sunday,  and I try to make most of the meetings they hold. People will tell me, "I went by and saw the statue. What can be done to help?"

In my town of Yeadon, they want to collect some money to give to the NLBPA, so that when the next project happens, like the upkeep and finishing of it, they'll be able to contribute. The town is struggling financially now—the taxes are awful—but they want to do what they can, and I like that.

There are plans for more attractions, and the old players are participating in that, too. We want to develop a Philadelphia Stars museum in the city. Of course, the contents are going to have to come from people like me who played, and those few who were close to it who are willing to part with their merchandise. And one day we *will* have that museum, if I live long enough!

Right now it's still in the talking stage. We're also hopeful that where the tennis courts now stand in Fairmount Park, we can build a completely enclosed Little League Baseball stadium. It will be a great thing for the city because then that area will also be a tourist spot. I think that statue was the beginning of a great intersection. It's really going to revitalize the whole neighborhood.

And another great thing is happening. The Philadelphia Phillies and Major League teams all across America have gotten involved in a teen program called Reviving Baseball in Inner Cities (RBI). It's trying to bring the neighborhood kids back to the fields so that they can teach them how to play baseball. Like I said, black kids just aren't interested in baseball much anymore, what with focusing on basketball and football.

The RBI program organizes sandlot teams and gets these children to start playing by their early teens. (They also have a Rookie League for kids 12 and under.) There's even an RBI World Series held in Major League baseball stadiums! By the time the kids that participate graduate from high school and go into college, they're going to be really good players. With any luck, the Phillies and other Major League teams will recruit the most promising ones.

None of this would be possible if it were not for Negro League Baseball, for which I am very pleased. Yes, it's all come more than 50 years late, but I'm glad God has let some of us live to see it, and I am sure there's more to come. I hope our children, their children, and those who are not yet born will keep black ball alive, too.

Afterword

I want to close this book with my thoughts about our society today and my hopes about the future. As I am a lay speaker for the United Methodist Church, I hope you'll forgive me if I take a moment to preach!

Sometimes I don't think America will ever get out of racism. It's a shame to say so. There are still places in the South where you're still not safe in your own home or walking down the street. Why, somebody just burned a cross on somebody's lawn in Georgia a few months back!

It's better than it used to be, but to overcome racism takes education. More than that, it will take some soul—searching and changing of the hearts and minds. Even if just one or two really fine people decide to help, they can start by talking about it with their friends.

As for larger activism, you can only get to that if you and your crowd are at least as large as the crowd that's doing the oppressing. If you don't have that groundswell of people, you'll never get what you want.

Surely the history of sports reflects the best and worst in us, and is part of the cure for our ills. What's more, sports are something we *need*.

For one thing, I firmly believe America has seen more progress in sports than in government. Think about it: Almost all of the Major League teams today are integrated. Name a sport—baseball, basketball, football, now golf and tennis, too—and instantly a list of black athletes comes to mind. Yet we have one black Supreme Court justice. And Clarence Thomas is black in color only—a real insider who I've heard is married to Barbara Bush's niece! (Now *that's* not something they usually tell you.) Attorney General Alberto Gonzalez was the first Latino to get that job, but that's probably because the Bush Administration is after the Hispanic votes. They're now the largest racial minority in this country, so that's probably the reason he is there.

What's more, I think politics is moving backward today. If we had the kind of Supreme Court in the '50s and '60s that we have had for the past decade, I don't think any of the civil rights laws would have gotten passed! These days, the government isn't in the business of making laws for the common person. It's mainly concerned with taking care of the super-rich. And if they don't like the laws that they're supposed to enforce, they just go in and try to change them.

All of these things take away from baseball, the game we love so well. That's why things like sports, which are less political and more personal, are going to help more with ending racism and other problems that hurt this country.

Do you remember 1994, the year we had no World Series because of a players' strike? Most of America was very angry and shocked. Something important was missing from our lives. It was almost as bad as closing down the government! Sports, and particularly baseball, have a way of satisfying our hearts and raising our spirits, and that enthusiasm is contagious! If not for sports and the sense of honest competition among the players it brings, and the love of the game by most customers, I think this nation might have a real civil uprising on its hands.

The world of baseball already knows this, and the world of football, basketball, and the Olympics do, too. Not one athlete, all over the world, would say any different. All of them want peace and a simple chance to compete in an athletic assembly. Win, lose, or draw, they accept the results and vow to be better the next time. These values remain after the games have ended, and form bonds among the players.

When they are greedy or arrogant, today's professional athletes play into the hands of those who would like baseball to return to the way it was 75 years ago. Having money is a must, but wealth cannot measure up to character. The "haves" have so much that they cannot live any better. The "have-nots" need so much and must rely on better choices, a better work ethic, live on the means they have, and trust in their gods to direct them.

Today we are in a state of mere survival. We must decide: What do we want— A vibrant America or one that languishes in hate and chaos? We are not in the darkness anymore; we can and do think for ourselves, so let's use our heads and our hearts to make the right decisions. It's time for truth and love to take the place of hate and racism.

It is not too late for reconciliation. We still have baseball and all the other sports. We still live in the best country in the world. There is a chance to make America a real second Promised Land. I believe we are religious enough, tolerant enough, economically sound enough, politically aware enough, and, well, *American* enough to realize this possibility. Let all people remember that we are our brothers' and sisters' keepers. Guns, jail, money, hate, attitude, and politics are not going to save America. Love will.

For all my nearly 80 years on earth, I know *I* plan to make the remainder of my years more fruitful—not only for me, but for all that I come in contact with. I refuse to hate anyone, for any reason. When I wake up in the morning and see the new day I feel blessed.

I've had a very good life. Certainly not a rich life, but I've got everything *but* money! That's why you'll often hear me say, "Don't let anybody take your joy away from you." Whatever else happens, if you lose your joy, you've got nothing.

I'd like to conclude with a special message to these children, just what I tell them when I speak to their classes. Live good lives and be good to each other and take care of each other. Every now and then when you run in the house, put your arms around your mom and give her a kiss. Look at the look on her face when you do that. You've made her happy. Your father's happy that you did it, too. And you know what? You've got a lot of joy deep down inside of you that you can't even explain.

Then maybe you should turn off the TV, go get yourself a ball, bat, and glove, and walk down to that nice field your town leaders built for you, or even that scruffy vacant lot with the cracked pavement. Bring your friends, even your parents, and start playing baseball again. You'll be glad you did!

Resources

There are a decent number of books and such about Negro League Baseball, but too many are somebody's opinion, or flat-out untrue. If you want more information about the Leagues, or a team, or an athlete, or any of the history, here are the most reliable sources I know of:

BOOKS

Only the Ball Was White: A History of Legendary Black Players and All-Black Professional Teams by Robert Peterson (published by Oxford University Press).

My Life in the Negro Leagues: An Autobiography by Wilmer Fields (published by Meckler Books).

ORGANIZATIONS

Negro League Baseball Players Association
610-284-6072
www.nlbpa.org

21st Century Radio (Dr. Bob Hieronimus)
Hieronimus & Co., Inc.
P.O. Box 648
Owings Mills, MD 21117 USA
(410) 356-4852
www.21stcenturyradio.com

MUSEUMS & DISPLAYS

Negro Leagues Baseball Museum
1616 E. 18th St.
Kansas City, MO 64108
816-221-1920
www.nlbm.com

National Baseball Hall of Fame
25 Main Street
Cooperstown, New York 13326
1-888-HALL-OF-FAME
www.baseballhalloffame.org

Philadelphia Stars Negro League Memorial Park
Corner of Parkside and Belmont Aves.
Philadelphia, PA 19131
215-879-8500 (Business Association of West Parkside)

Sports Legends at Camden Yards
301 W. Camden St.
Camden Station
Baltimore, MD 21201
410-727-1539

PEOPLE

Feel free to contact me and I'll do my best to see you get the information you need.

Stanley Glenn, NLBPA President
9 Baily Rd.
Yeadon, PA 19050
610-284-6072